H6K "MAVIS"/H8K "EMILY"
VS
PB4Y-1/2 LIBERATOR/PRIVATEER

Pacific Theater 1943–45

EDWARD M. YOUNG

OSPREY PUBLISHING

Bloomsbury Publishing Plc

Kemp House, Chawley Park, Cumnor Hill, Oxford, OX2 9PH, UK

29 Earlsfort Terrace, Dublin 2, Ireland

1385 Broadway, 5th Floor, New York, NY 10018, USA

E-mail; info@ospreypublishing.com

www.ospreypublishing.com

OSPREY is a trademark of Osprey Publishing Ltd

First published in Great Britain in 2023

© Osprey Publishing Ltd, 2023

A catalog record for this book is available from the British Library.

ISBN: PB 9781472852502; eBook 9781472852496; ePDF 9781472852526; XML 9781472852519

23 24 25 26 27   10 9 8 7 6 5 4 3 2 1

Edited by Tony Holmes

Cover artworks and battlescene by Gareth Hector

Three-views, cockpit and turret views, Engaging the Enemy and armament artwork by Jim Laurier

Index by Fionbar Lyons

Originated by PDQ Digital Media Solutions, UK

Printed and bound in India by Replika Press Private Ltd.

Osprey Publishing supports the Woodland Trust, the UK's leading woodland conservation charity.

To find out more about our authors and books visit **www.ospreypublishing.com**. Here you will find extracts, author interviews, details of forthcoming events and the option to sign up for our newsletter.

Acknowledgements

I would again like to thank my good friend Osamu Tagaya for so generously sharing his knowledge and insights into Imperial Japanese Naval Air Force (IJNAF) operations during World War II. Michael Claringbould kindly identified the likely unit for the first Type 97 "Mavis" shot down by a PB4Y-1. Ms. Takako Owada translated several Japanese language materials for me. The photographs for this volume came from several sources. I would especially like to thank Ms. Holly Reed and her always helpful staff in the Still Pictures Reference at the National Archives and Records Administration at College Park, Maryland. My thanks to Ms. Nicole Davis at the Museum of Flight, Ms. Debbie Seracini at the San Diego Air & Space Museum, Ms. Seiko Sugiyama at the Yamato Museum in Kure, Japan, and Ms. Naoko Hara at ShinMaywa Industries, Ltd. for providing photographs from their collections. It is always a great pleasure to work with two such exceptionally talented artists as Gareth Hector and Jim Laurier. My thanks to both gentlemen for their ability to turn my ideas into excellent illustrations. Finally, my thanks to Tony Holmes for his support for this volume on a rare aspect of the air war over the Pacific.

H6K "Mavis" cover art

By the time VB-104 arrived on Guadalcanal in mid-August 1943, the IJNAF had withdrawn the H6K from frontline patrol operations after the type had proved vulnerable to Allied fighters. The "Mavis'" range made it an effective long-range transport to carry personnel and supplies to Japan's far-flung bases over its newly conquered and greatly expanded empire. The transport version, designated the H6K4-L, had all armament removed, cabins installed for up to 18 passengers and cargo compartments in the bow and stern. The defenseless transport was, however, easy prey for the heavily armed PB4Y-1, which had a considerable speed advantage. Without gun turrets, it was difficult for an H6K4-L to keep a sharp lookout for American patrol aircraft, and once attacked, there was little the "Mavis" pilot could do to escape. Lacking self-sealing fuel tanks, the H6K4-L inevitably burst into flames when its engines and wings were hit during an attack, dooming the flying boat to destruction.

PB4Y-1 Liberator cover art

The first encounter between a US Navy PB4Y-1 Liberator and an IJNAF flying boat took place on August 28, 1943. VB-104 had started to arrive on Guadalcanal on August 19 to replace VB-101, taking on responsibility for patrolling the areas north, northeast and west of the Solomon Islands. Lt John Alley and his crew were nearing the end of their patrol sector when they sighted a H6K "Mavis" flying above them on a course for Rabaul. Alley climbed up to attack, unaware that the aircraft he was approaching was a transport version likely assigned to the 11th Koku Sentai. The PB4Y's gunners opened fire when the "Mavis" was 500 yards away, the bow turret gunner expending 200 rounds and hitting the flying boat's Nos. 3 and 4 engines. Soon the starboard wing was in flames, and the "Mavis" nosed over and crashed into the sea.

Previous Page

Lt Stoughton Atwood and his crew made VB-115's second claim for an "Emily" destroyed on July 2, 1944 during a patrol southwest of Palau, in Micronesia. Atwood flew past the flying boat after his gunners had knocked out its tail and dorsal turrets, getting some close-up photographs of the H8K before it descended on fire. (Record Group 80G-241258, RG80, Still Pictures Branch, National Archives and Records Administration (NARA))

CONTENTS

INTRODUCTION

During World War II, air combats between large, four-engined aircraft were a comparatively rare occurrence. Allied and Axis bombers had few opportunities for such encounters, but there were clashes between maritime patrol aircraft. These aerial engagements are unique in the annals of air warfare. Patrol aircraft most often faced enemy single- and twin-engined fighters, but there were occasions where rival maritime machines encountered each other during their patrols.

In the early years of the war the Luftwaffe's Fw 200 Condors of *Kampfgeschwader* (KG) 40 engaged in combat with RAF Coastal Command Hudson, Sunderland, and Whitley aircraft, claiming two of the latter shot down and losing a Condor to a Hudson of No. 233 Sqn. During July–August 1943, KG 40 Condors ran into US Army Air Force (USAAF) anti-submarine squadron B-24Ds over the Bay of Biscay, losing three Condors to the heavily armed Liberators. Later that year US Navy PB4Y squadron VB-110 claimed an He 177 bomber.

However, it was over the vast Pacific Ocean where most of these clashes took place. From August 1943 until the final combat in May 1945, aggressive PB4Y Liberators, the US Navy's designation for the B-24, shot down 15 Imperial Japanese Naval Air Force (IJNAF) Kawanishi H6K "Mavis" and Kawanishi H8K "Emily" flying boats without loss – a remarkable record.

The primary mission of maritime patrol aircraft was reconnaissance; offensive operations were secondary. Intelligence on an enemy's location, disposition, and composition of forces is vital to a military commander on land or sea. As Rear Admiral John S. McCain, commanding the Aircraft Scouting Force for the US Navy's Atlantic Fleet, wrote in January 1942:

Information is without doubt the most important service required by a fleet commander. Accurate, complete and up to the minute knowledge of the position, strength, and movement of enemy forces is very difficult to obtain under war conditions. If these facts are made available while the enemy is at a great distance from our shores and similar information about our own forces is denied the enemy, the commander is given time to plan his movements and select the time and position of contact in such a manner that he may operate under a tactical advantage.

In the age of sail the fast frigate scouted the oceans for the enemy fleet, a role the cruiser took on as steam replaced sail in the world's navies. Aircraft brought about a radical change in naval reconnaissance capabilities, as they were faster than any surface ship and could cover a far greater distance in a shorter amount of time, and with radio communications they could pass on intelligence immediately to the commander of the fleet. During the interwar years, both the IJNAF and the US Navy recognized the necessity of having an aircraft capable of performing long-range ocean reconnaissance. Both forces developed the large, multi-engined flying boat in response to this need. As Rear Admiral McCain wrote:

> For the source of this most important information, the fleet commanders have come to rely more and more on the patrol plane. With their normal and advanced bases strategically located, surprise contacts between major forces can hardly occur. In addition to receiving contact reports on enemy forces in vital areas, the patrol planes, due to their great endurance, can shadow and track these forces, keeping the fleet commander informed of their every movement.

The long-range flying boat provided a solution to a problem that confronted both the Imperial Japanese Navy (IJN) and the US Navy – the vast expanse of the Pacific Ocean.

War Plan Orange, as devised by the Joint Army and Navy Board in the interwar years should conflict erupt with Japan, envisioned the US Navy's Pacific Fleet

Having been the commander of the Atlantic Fleet's Aircraft Scouting Force in 1941–42, Vice-Admiral John S. McCain was fully aware of the importance of land-based multi-engined patrol aircraft when it came to performing long-range ocean reconnaissance. (US Navy)

The Consolidated Aircraft Company's P2Y was a development of its earlier XPY-1, and it served in the US Navy's patrol squadrons until replaced by the company's PBY Catalina from 1937. Ironically, Kawanishi acquired a P2Y-1 for the IJNAF to evaluate. (NH-94803, Naval History and Heritage Command (NHHC))

making a westward advance from Hawaii to reinforce or recapture the Philippines and Guam – both American possessions. A US fleet advancing westward, as well as America's few island bases, could potentially come under attack from any direction. An enemy carrier force, which could travel hundreds of miles overnight, made the risk of attack, and the need for adequate reconnaissance, even greater. The US Navy needed patrol aircraft that could range out upwards of 1,000 miles beyond the fleet.

An interwar struggle over which service, the US Navy or the US Army, had responsibility for employing land-based strike aircraft in coastal defense ended in favor of the US Army Air Corps (USAAC) and restricted the US Navy's acquisition of land-based patrol aircraft until just before America's entry into World War II. As a result, the US Navy relied exclusively on flying boats for long-range over-water reconnaissance, primarily fielding aircraft designed by the Consolidated Aircraft Company (specifically the P2Y, which was replaced by the PBY from 1937) and the Glenn Martin Company, and using seaplane tenders in lieu of advanced land bases.

The IJN's strategy in the event of war with America envisioned engaging the US Pacific Fleet in a decisive naval battle in closer proximity to Japan. The IJN recognized that its fleet would be numerically inferior to a US Navy fleet, partly due to America's greater resources but also because of restrictions on fleet size and composition imposed on Japan by the naval treaties of the 1920s and 1930s. To have a chance of success, the IJN needed to whittle down the Pacific Fleet through a campaign of attrition as it sailed westward from Hawaii. Reconnaissance, locating, and tracking the movements of the Pacific Fleet, was vital to this strategy.

As an island nation, Japan faced approaches to the home islands from multiple directions. Having acquired the former German possessions of the Marianas, Marshall, and Caroline islands in the wake of World War I, changes under a League of Nations Mandate gave the IJN a potential string of bases across a large span of the Pacific Ocean. Although Japan had agreed not to fortify these islands, flying boats and their attendant seaplane tenders had the ability to rapidly advance from the home islands to the island chains in the event of war without the need for land-based facilities. This need for long-range reconnaissance on the part of both navies set the stage for the wartime encounters between patrolling aircraft.

While reconnaissance was the primary mission for maritime patrol aircraft in the event of war, the IJN and the US Navy ensured that their long-range flying boats had an offensive capability as well. Both navies envisioned using these aircraft for offensive missions and ensured that they could carry a range of bombs and torpedoes. Early in the war the Japanese flying boats undertook several bombing missions, including a raid on Pearl Harbor, but it was the US Navy, once it was finally able to acquire land-based medium and heavy bombers, which would revolutionize the role of maritime patrol aircraft.

Flown by aggressive young pilots, these land-based aircraft would bomb Japanese bases on islands across the Pacific, attack Japanese shipping, and pursue IJNAF aircraft. In these aerial battles, the US Navy's PB4Y-1 Liberator and PB4Y-2 Privateer would claim more than 300 Japanese aircraft destroyed and achieve a 10.9-to-one victory-to-loss ratio – a figure higher than any other land-based US Navy or US Marine Corps aircraft.

CHRONOLOGY

1934

Spring (early) IJN issues Experimental 9-Shi Large Flying Boat specification to the Kawanishi Kokuki KK (Kawanishi Aircraft Company, Ltd.).

1936

July 14 Kawanishi H6K1 Flying Boat makes its first flight.

1938

January The re-engined first, third, and fourth prototypes enter IJNAF service as the Type 97 Flying Boat Model 1 (H6K1), with the aircraft being placed in full production.

August Kawanishi begins work on the Navy Experimental 13-Shi Large Flying Boat intended as a replacement for the H6K.

1939

January Consolidated Aircraft begins work on the Model 32 bomber.

March 30 USAAC awards Consolidated a contract for the XB-24 prototype.

Spring (early) Production of the Type 97 Flying Boat initiated with ten pre-production aircraft designated the Type 97 Navy Flying Boat Model 2 (H6K2) and the first production version designated the Type 97 Navy Flying Boat Model 22 (H6K4). The H6K enters service with the Yokohama Kokutai (air group).

April 27 USAAC orders seven YB-24s.

August 10 USAAC orders 38 B-24As.

December 29 First flight of the XB-24.

1940

April H6Ks commence flying long-range maritime reconnaissance missions.

August USAAC orders 408 B-24s.

December 31 Prototype of the Navy Experimental 13-Shi Large Flying Boat, designated H8K1, completed.

1941

January Prototype H8K1 makes its maiden flight.

Fall H8K1 accepted for service as the Navy Type 2 Flying Boat Model 1-1.

December 7 IJNAF carriers strike Pearl Harbor.

1942

January– February H6K4s based at Truk conduct bombing raids on Rabaul, the Dutch East Indies, and Port Moresby in New Guinea.

March 4 Two pre-production H8Ks attempt to bomb Pearl Harbor but are thwarted by cloud cover over their target.

May– September H6Ks and H8Ks support IJN operations during the Battle of Midway and advances in the Solomon Islands.

July 7 USAAF agrees to allow the US Navy to acquire land-based bombers, including the B-24D as the PB4Y-1.

August 7 US Marines land on Guadalcanal.

September 1 First two PB4Y-1s delivered to the US Navy for test purposes.

October Seventeen PB4Y-1s delivered to the US Navy for installation of naval equipment and assignment to patrol squadrons. VP-51 becomes the first US Navy patrol squadron to convert to the PB4Y-1.

1943

January VP-51 arrives on Guadalcanal, becoming the first PB4Y-1 squadron in the Southwest Pacific. It is re-designated VB-101 the following month.

April Bureau of Aeronautics meets with Consolidated to discuss modifications to the B-24.

May Bureau of Aeronautics requests three prototypes of the PB4Y-2.

August VB-104 arrives on Guadalcanal.

August 28 Lt Charles J. Alley and his crew of VB-104 shoot down a "Mavis" for the PB4Y's first claim against an IJNAF flying boat.

September 30 Prototype XPB4Y-2 makes first flight.

October VB-106 arrives on Midway, thus becoming the first PB4Y-1 squadron in the Central Pacific.

November VB-108 arrives on the Ellice Islands, south of the Gilbert Islands.

November 20 Operation *Galvanic* (occupation of the Gilbert Islands) commences with landings on Tarawa.

December 2 Lt William J. Graham and crew of VB-108 claim the first "Emily" shot down by a PB4Y-1.

1944

February 1 Invasion of the Marshall Islands. US Marines and US Army forces land on Roi, Namur, and Kwajalein.

February 19 US Marines land on Eniwetok, continuing the capture of the Marshall Islands.

March–May Westward advance of US Navy patrol squadrons continues. VB-108 and VB-109 move to Kwajalein and VB-106 moves to Nadzab, in New Guinea. Other units move to Los Negros, in the Admiralty Islands.

April 17 Lt Everett Mitchell and crew of VB-106, now based at Nadzab, shoot down a "Mavis."

April 24 Lt Everett Mitchell and crew of VB-106, now flying from Los Negros, intercept and shoot down an "Emily" for their second Japanese flying boat victory in a week.

May–July From May 7 to July 2, PB4Y squadrons in the Southwest and Central Pacific shoot down a "Mavis" and four "Emily" flying boats.

June 15 Invasion of the Marianas begins with landings on Saipan (Operation *Forager*).

July 21 American forces land on Guam.

July 24 American forces land on Tinian.

August VB-102 and VB-116 move to Tinian.

August VPB-118 and VPB-119 are the first squadrons to convert to the PB4Y-2.

October 1 All US Navy multi-engined VB squadrons re-designated VPB for Patrol Bombing.

October 20 US Army troops land on Leyte, in the Philippines.

December VPB-104 and VPB-117 move to Tacloban airfield on Leyte. That month VPB-104 shoots down a "Mavis" and VPB-117 claims an "Emily."

1945

January 6 VPB-118 arrives on Tinian with PB4Y-2s.

March 11 VPB-118 shoots down an "Emily" for the first and only victory over an IJNAF flying boat by a PB4Y-2.

March 17 VPB-104 shoots down an "Emily" for the squadron's third victory over a Japanese flying boat – the most for any PB4Y squadron.

March IJN Ministry orders an end to production of flying boats.

May 9 Flying from Iwo Jima, VPB-116's squadron commander shoots down a "Mavis" for the final PB4Y victory over an IJNAF flying boat.

DESIGN AND DEVELOPMENT

KAWANISHI TYPE 97 FLYING BOAT (H6K)

In the aftermath of World War I, the IJN requested British technical assistance to advance the state of Japanese naval aviation. The resulting British Air Mission, as it was called, became known as the Sempill Mission after its leader, the Master of Sempill. The mission brought with it many naval aircraft of varying types, including 15 Felixstowe F.5 flying boats – the first of their type demonstrated to the IJN. The latter decided to adopt the F.5 as its standard long-range patrol aircraft, and with assistance from Short Brothers, began building the F.5 in Japan, initially at the Yokosuka Naval Arsenal, then at the Hiro Naval Arsenal, with an additional 40 built by the Aichi Aircraft Company, Ltd.

Toward the end of 1927, the Hiro Naval Arsenal completed a prototype of a replacement for the F.5 which, after testing, entered service with the IJNAF as the Type 15-1 Flying Boat (H1H1). Aside from examples built at the Hiro Naval Arsenal, H1H1s were also constructed by the Aichi Aircraft Company. The Type 15 served as the IJNAF's principal flying boat into the late 1930s.

In 1930, the Hiro Naval Arsenal completed a prototype of a new flying boat with an all-metal hull based on a Supermarine Southampton flying boat imported for study in Japan. The IJNAF adopted this model as the Type 89 Flying Boat (H2H1). To help

9

The Type 15 (H1H1 to H1H3) was the IJNAF's principal flying boat until 1938, with 20 aircraft built at the IJN's Hiro and Yokosuka Naval Arsenals and an additional 45 completed by the Aichi Aircraft Company. (2008-3-31_image_529_01, Peter M. Bowers Collection, Museum of Flight (MoF))

build the 13 aircraft ordered from the Hiro Naval Arsenal, the IJNAF contracted with Kawanishi Kokuki K.K. (Kawanishi Aircraft Company, Ltd.) to fabricate components for the Type 89.

Established in 1921, Kawanishi had built several types of single-engined aircraft, including seaplanes, but the Type 89 was the company's first exercise in working on a large multi-engined machine. At the same time, however, the IJNAF had also contracted with Kawanishi to design and build a large, three-engined flying boat. Company engineers worked closely with Short Brothers on the aircraft, which was based on the British firm's Calcutta and Singapore flying boats, with the prototype built in Rochester, Kent, and shipped to Japan.

Having obtained a license for its production, Kawanishi completed the first prototype in 1931 and a second aircraft, designated the Type F, a year later. After evaluating the prototypes, the IJNAF accepted the Kawanishi aircraft as the Type 90 Model 2 Flying Boat (H3K1), the first Japanese military aircraft to feature a tail turret. Kawanishi completed two more Type 90-2 Flying Boats, one of which made a 1,496-mile flight from Japan to Saipan, demonstrating its capabilities as a long-range patrol aircraft. Although this was an impressive feat, performance of the Type 90

Kawanishi obtained a license from Short Brothers to build a large, three-engined flying boat based on its Singapore and Calcutta designs. Kawanishi completed four aircraft as the Type 90-2 Flying Boat (H3K1). The experience its engineers gained during the construction of the Type 90-2s provided the foundation for the company's later Type 97 and Type 2 flying boats. (2008-3-31_image_529_04, Peter M. Bowers Collection, MoF)

Model 2 did not meet the IJNAF's expectations and did not go into production. Nevertheless, the effort helped establish Kawanishi's reputation as a builder of large flying boats.

During 1933, in response to the IJNAF's 8-Shi (based on the reign year of the Showa emperor) requirement for a flying boat with better performance than the Type 90 Model 2, Kawanishi conducted extensive testing in wind tunnels and water tanks of two monoplane flying boat designs, with the company's designations Type Q for a four-engined design and Type R for a three-engined design. The IJNAF chose not to pursue either of these, and instead, in 1934, issued its 9-Shi Experimental Large Flying Boat requirement to Kawanishi with a demanding set of specifications. The IJNAF wanted a cruising speed of 138mph, with a range of 2,871 miles carrying up to 2,000lb of bombs or two 1,764lb torpedoes – a performance superior to almost all British or American military or commercial flying boats of the period.

Dr. Shizuo Kikuhara, Kawanishi's chief designer of the 9-shi Ogata Hiko Tei (Large Body Flying Boat Prototype 9), chose a long, slim and compact hull which rose gracefully to a twin tail incorporating a gun turret. A long-span parasol wing, longer than any contemporary foreign flying boat wing, had three spars. For additional strength, it contained a span-wise corrugated inner metal sheet covered with an outer smooth metal skin. Two inverted V-shaped struts attached the wing to the fuselage, with additional bracing struts attached to the hull and extending to the mid-span of the wing. Four Nakajima Hikari 2 nine-cylinder air-cooled, radial engines, set in the leading edge of the wing well above the ocean spray, provided 840hp each for take-off.

The 9-Shi prototype (designated the Type S in Kawanishi's system) had accommodation for a crew of eight, with a pilot and co-pilot sat side-by-side, an aircraft commander just behind the pilots, an observer in the bow and a flight engineer, radio operator, navigator, and reserve crewman in the aft section. Initial armament was three 7.7mm machine guns, one in the tail turret, one in a powered dorsal turret, and one in an open bow position.

The Type S prototype made its first flight in July 1936 and met the required specifications, although the IJNAF decided to replace the Nakajima Hikari 2 engines

The 9-Shi Experimental Large Flying Boat, which served as the prototype for the Type 97 flying boat series and entered service as the H6K1. Note the 1,764lb aerial torpedo attached to the port wing struts. This mounting could also carry three or six 132lb bombs. (2008-3-31_image_503_01, Peter M. Bowers Collection, MoF)

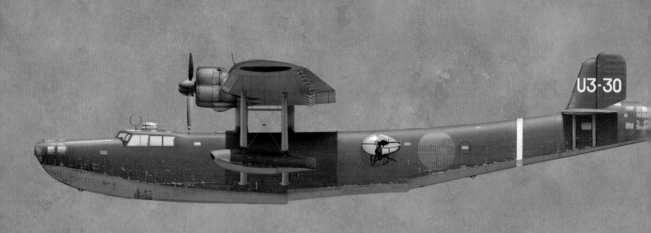

H6K5 "MAVIS"

This Type 97 Flying Boat, coded "U3-30," was a Model 23 (H6K5), the last version of the Type 97 built by Kawanishi. The aircraft was assigned to the 801st Kokutai, based on Hokkaido, in November 1943. The Model 23 had more powerful Mitsubishi Kinsei 53 engines offering 1,300hp for take-off, and replaced the open bow gun position with a small turret atop the cockpit. Kawanishi built 36 Model 23s before ending production of the Type 97.

with more powerful Mitsubishi Kinsei 43 14-cylinder air-cooled radial engines offering 1,000hp for take-off.

During 1937 the first and second prototypes were handed over to the IJNAF for operational testing with the Yokohama Kokutai. At the conclusion of the test period in early 1938, the IJNAF adopted the Type S as the Type 97 Flying Boat Model 1 (H6K1) and ordered it into production, with the first ten examples designated the Type 97 Flying Boat (H6K2). The first model built in quantity was the Type 97 Model 2-2 (H6K4), which incorporated several changes. Larger fuel tanks extended the Type 97's maximum range to 3,378 miles. An open cockpit for a 7.7mm Type 92 machine gun replaced the dorsal turret, with two similar weapons placed in blisters on either side of the fuselage behind the wing. Finally, a redesigned tail turret accommodated a Type 99 20mm cannon. The H6K4 model progressively equipped IJNAF flying boat Kokutai in both Japan and Taiwan. At the start of the Pacific War there were 66 H6Ks operational, principally in two flying boat Kokutai.

Kawanishi also built a transport version of the H6K for the Dai Nippon Koku K.K. (Dai Nippon Airways), which operated a service from Japan to Micronesia via Saipan, in the Marianas. The airline received two early models, designated H6K2-L, and later 16 more based on the H6K4 as the H6K4-L, while the IJNAF also acquired 20 H6K4-Ls.

The last version of the H6K, completed during 1941, featured more powerful engines and higher maximum and cruising speeds. Designated the Type 97 Model 23 (H6K5), 36 aircraft went to the IJNAF's flying boat Kokutai. Series production of the H6K began at Kawanishi's Nauro factory near the city of Kobe in 1939, and the flying boats were built exclusively in this factory until production ceased in April 1943.

A formation of H6K2s from an unidentified IJNAF Kokutai. The H6K2 was the first production version of the Type 97 to enter service, followed by the H6K4, which added gun blisters on either side of the fuselage for the Type 92 7.7mm machine guns and replaced the dorsal turret with an open gun position. (Record Group 80G-169790, Still Pictures Branch, National Archives and Records Administration (NARA))

KAWANISHI TYPE 2 FLYING BOAT (H8K)

Just seven months after adopting the Type 97 Flying Boat, the IJNAF issued a new directive to Kawanishi in August 1938 to begin designing a successor under the Shi-13 Ogata Hiko Tei (Large Flying Boat Prototype No. 13) program. Once again, the IJNAF presented Kawanishi with a demanding set of specifications. The new design was to have a maximum speed of 276mph and a cruising speed of 184mph, while range on a reconnaissance mission was to be 4,600 miles – a considerable advance on the H6K, as well as the new generation of flying boats under development in Britain and the USA. In Britain the new Short Sunderland had just entered service, while the US Navy was evaluating the large Consolidated XPB2Y-1 and Sikorsky XPBS-1 flying boats.

The IJNAF wanted a flying boat that would also have a powerful defensive armament with turreted 20mm cannon in addition to 7.7mm machine guns, and a bomb load of up to 4,000lb. The challenge for Kawanishi's design staff, again under the leadership of Dr. Shizuo Kikuhara, was to develop a design that would meet the IJNAF's requirements for cruising range and still boast a high cruising speed. A larger wing improved range, but the increase in drag would reduce cruising speed.

The Kawanishi designers chose a shoulder-mounted cantilever wing as a better alternative to the H6K's parasol wing. This reduced parasite drag, which offset the increase in weight of the wing. New, lighter weight duralumin spars helped lower the

13

The Kawanishi Experimental 13-Shi Flying Boat photographed in Kobe harbor during testing in early 1941. The aircraft is seen making trial take-off runs after company engineers had added spray suppression strips along the lower fuselage. (2008-3-31_image_511_01, Peter M. Bowers Collection, MoF)

OPPOSITE

This aircraft, "51-085," was a late production H8K2 assigned to the 851st Kokutai for patrol missions over the Central Pacific. With this model, the IJNAF replaced the gun blisters on the sides of the fuselage behind the wing trailing edge with flat, rectangular windows. The late model Type 2 Flying Boats had the Type 3 Mark 6 (Type H6) airborne search radar the IJNAF developed specifically for large aircraft. This radar had Yagi antennas on either side of the forward fuselage, and the system could detect a large warship at a range of approximately 168 miles using a wave length of two meters. This particular aircraft had the misfortune to encounter a VB-115 PB4Y-1 on July 2, 1944, and it was shot down with the loss of its entire crew.

weight of the wing structure, and for strength, Kawanishi used the same combination of a corrugated inner skin with a flat metal plate covering for the wing. Company engineers developed a special Fowler-type flap to reduce landing speed. To improve aerodynamic performance, the fuselage had as narrow a beam, or hull width, as possible and a larger length-to-beam ratio than previous flying boats. A taller fuselage provided space for crew and equipment, the height being equal to the distance from the bottom of the fuselage to the top of the wing on the H6K. While this improved air speed, it led to certain hydrodynamic problems. The new design used the same bottom hull shape and floats as the H6K.

The 13-Shi flying boat prototype had, for the time, a powerful armament. The electrically-operated spherical bow turret held a Type 99 20mm cannon, with a second such weapon in a dorsal blister turret and 20mm cannon in each of the waist blisters, making this the most heavily armed flying boat yet designed. A tail turret held a Type 92 7.7mm machine gun, with a second 7.7mm weapon in a ventral hatch below the tail assembly. There were hatches for additional 7.7mm machine guns behind the pilots' seats on the flightdeck. The Type 2 had provision for carrying bombs and torpedoes externally beneath the wings between the inner and outer engine nacelles. To provide the flying boat with its impressive range, the machine had six main fuel tanks in the lower hull and eight additional tanks placed in the central part of the wing.

What made the 13-Shi prototype's superior performance possible was a new, powerful 14-cylinder air-cooled radial engine developed by the Aero Engine Department of Mitsubishi Jukogyo K.K. (Mitsubishi Heavy Industries, Ltd.). Based on the experimental A10 (Ha-18) engine, the Kasei 11 (designated the MK4A by the IJNAF), produced 1,530hp for take-off. When Kawanishi began work on the 13-Shi project, the Kasei 11 was close to production, so the design team had no hesitation in adopting this engine for the prototype. The latter was completed at the end of December 1940, with flight testing beginning immediately, such was the IJNAF's urgency to get the new flying boat into service.

Flight tests revealed that in the air, the 13-Shi prototype demonstrated acceptable flying characteristics. However, handling problems arose during taxiing at high speed and take-off, with spray being thrown up into the propellers. In an effort to eradicate this issue, Kawanishi engineers raised the depth of the hull by 19.6 inches and installed

H8K2 "EMILY"

92ft 3in.

30ft 0in.

124ft 8in.

51-085

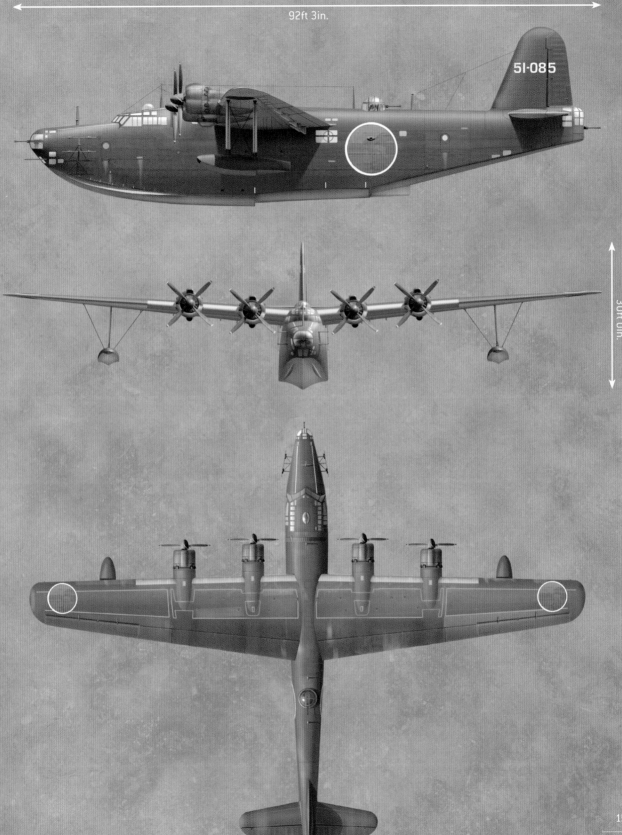

The second prototype of the 13-Shi Flying Boat, the first H8K1 series, with a revised rudder shape, deeper fuselage, and an extended nose to incorporate a gun turret for the Type 99 20mm cannon. Early-production H8K1s can be seen under construction behind the prototype. (2008-3-31_image_512_01, Peter M. Bowers Collection, MoF)

special strips along the front of the fuselage to deflect the spray from the propellers. The prototype also tended to porpoise as speed increased on take-off, but the Kawanishi test pilots found that if they maintained an angle of attack of five degrees they could control this tendency.

Additional prototypes built during 1941 featured a lengthened bow, modified vertical tail surfaces, and Mitsubishi MK4B Kasei 12 engines. In February 1942 the IJNAF officially adopted the new flying boat as the Type 2 Flying Boat Model 11 (H8K1), with two of the prototypes making the aircraft's combat debut the following month in an unsuccessful attack on Pearl Harbor.

As more operational pilots began flying the H8K, the porpoising problem re-emerged. Pilots transitioning from the H6K found sitting in the much higher fuselage of the H8K and the flying boat's slanting nose made it difficult to correctly judge the angle of attack relative to the horizon, and thus stay within the five degrees specified in the aircraft's operating manual. Kawanishi engineers solved the problem by installing a thin horizontal stick, nicknamed "kanzashi" (the ornamental hairpin worn by Japanese women that the stick resembled), below the pitot tube on the nose that lined up with the horizon as seen from the pilot's seat when the angle of attack reached five degrees, and added a white graduation mark on the front of the windscreen to help the pilot maintain the correct angle of attack.

Production of the Type 2 Flying Boat Model 11 ended after Kawanishi had completed 12 production aircraft. The 18th aircraft became the Type 2 Flying Boat Model 12 (H8K2) when the IJNAF changed the engines to the more powerful Mitsubishi Kasei MK4Q Model 22, which gave 1,850hp. The Kasei Model 22 gave a higher maximum speed with a small reduction in range on reconnaissance missions. The H8K2 had a revised armament, with a Type 99 20mm cannon replacing the 7.7mm machine guns in the tail turret; later production models had a revised dorsal turret. Uniquely for a Japanese aircraft at the time, and following heavy losses of H6Ks in combat with American fighters in the battles around the Solomons, the IJNAF installed protected fuel tanks and armor protection for the crew in the H8K2.

The IJNAF had recognized that the H8K's large and deep fuselage would be useful for carrying passengers and cargo. In 1943 it instructed Kawanishi to develop a transport version of the aircraft, as the company had done with the H6K. Kawanishi

modified the first 13-Shi prototype to incorporate five passenger compartments that could hold 41 passengers normally and a maximum of 64. It removed the dorsal and waist blister turrets, leaving one 13mm machine gun in the bow and the 20mm cannon in the tail turret, and installed windows along the sides of the fuselage. The IJNAF ordered Kawanishi to begin production of this version as the Type 2 Transport Flying Boat Model 23 (H8K2-L), later changing the designation to Transport Flying Boat Seiku (Clear Sky) Type 32. During the war Kawanishi built 36 transport versions.

To increase the speed of the H8K, the IJNAF resurrected an earlier idea of installing retractable floats – something it had previously abandoned in order to save weight. Kawanishi built two prototypes as the Type 2 Flying Boat Model 22 (H8K3) and undertook extensive flight tests, but this model never went into production. In 1945 these two aircraft were re-engined with Mitsubishi MK4T-B Kasei 25b engines of 1,825hp as the Type 2 Flying Boat Model 23 (H8K4), but the IJNAF did not pursue further development.

Production of the H8K built up slowly, with Kawanishi's Nauro factory near Kobe completing 11 aircraft during 1942. After manufacturing three flying boats at Nauro in early 1943, Kawanishi shifted production to its nearby Konan plant, which built the majority of the H8Ks. The Konan factory completed its first Type 2 aircraft in February 1943, and by the end of the year had raised production to ten aircraft a month, completing 63 during 1943. Production increased to 77 H8Ks during 1944, then fell sharply in 1945 to just ten aircraft when the Navy Ministry cancelled production of flying boats in favor of Kawanishi's N1K2-J fighter.

The H8K replaced the H6K in frontline flying boat units as rapidly as production would allow. IJNAF pilots considered it to be a very good aircraft, appreciating its ability to quickly lift off from the water and climb at a steep angle. The H8K was not hard to maneuver thanks to it possessing good rudder control. The aircraft's top speed of 290mph was also appreciably higher than the H6K's 211mph.

This late production H8K2 was found by US servicemen after the end of the war, its propellers having been removed as ordered by the victorious Allies. The aircraft belonged to the Yokosuka Kokutai based near Yokohama, south of Tokyo, and it underwent a detailed examination by the Allied Air Technical Intelligence Unit. (GAF_image_803_1, MoF)

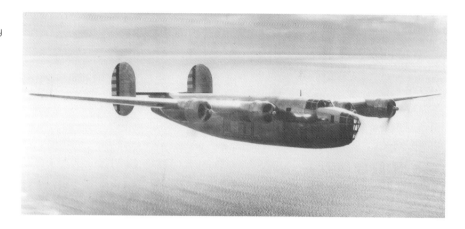

The Consolidated XB-24 flying along the California coast in early 1940. To boost the bomber's speed, the USAAC had the manufacturer fit turbo-superchargers to the XB-24's four Pratt & Whitney R-1830-33 Twin Wasp engines. (RG342, 3B-25234, NARA)

CONSOLIDATED PB4Y-1 LIBERATOR AND PB4Y-2 PRIVATEER

OPPOSITE

PB4Y-1 BuNo 38889 was a J-model Liberator (USAAF serial number 44-41246) serving with VPB-104 at Tacloban, on the island of Leyte in the Philippines, along with VPB-117 and detachments from VPB-101 in December 1944. At the time, VPB-104's CO ordered his crews to remove any nose art from their aircraft such as victory markings so that if they were shot down they could tell their Japanese captors they were simply new replacements. Lt Paul Stevens and his crew used BuNo 38889 to shoot down three of the six Japanese aircraft they claimed between December 1944 and March 1945. Their first victory was a D3A "Val" on December 31, 1944, followed by a second "Val" in February 1945 and an E16A "Paul" floatplane on March 4, 1945. Stevens and his crew claimed three more aerial victories that month, with a third "Val" on March 10 and an E13A1 "Jake" floatplane and an H8K "Emily" one week later.

During 1941, the US Navy looked to extend the coverage of America's Atlantic Neutrality Patrol by flying from bases in Argentia, in Newfoundland, and Iceland, where the severe weather and cold temperatures made the operation of its PBY flying boats and their seaplane tenders difficult. It was clear the US Navy needed land-based aircraft. However, for years the War Department had successfully denied it land-based aircraft due to the jurisdictional disagreement over who was responsible for coastal defense.

Finally, in October 1941, the US Navy obtained 20 USAAC Lockheed A-29 Hudsons as PBO-1s and assigned them to VP-82 at Argentia as its first land-based patrol squadron. Reports from Britain on the successful employment of B-24 bombers as long-range anti-submarine aircraft by RAF Coastal Command convinced the US Navy that land-based patrol bombers were not only better suited to operations over the North Atlantic than its flying boats, they also had superior performance over the latter, with heavier armament and bomb loads.

In early 1942 the US Navy requested an allocation of B-24 bombers from the USAAC, only to have the request refused. After intensive negotiations, the US Navy reached an agreement with the War Department on July 7, 1942 that in return for getting B-24s, it would cancel its contract with Boeing for the PBB-1 Sea Ranger twin-engined flying boat and turn the company's Renton factory over to production of the Boeing B-29 for the USAAF.

After obtaining two B-24Ds for test purposes, the US Navy subsequently acquired eight D-models in September 1942, designating them PB4Y-1s. More Liberators followed during 1943. The US Navy ultimately received 977 PB4Y-1s in total, consisting of 278 B-24Ds, 368 B-24Js, 186 B-24Ls, and 145 B-24Ms. US Marine Corps photographic reconnaissance squadron VMD-254 was the first unit to take the PB4Y-1 to war, moving to the South Pacific in October 1942, followed by VP-51 (soon re-designated VB-101) in January 1943. By the end of 1943 the US Navy had 12 PB4Y-1 squadrons operating in the Atlantic and the Pacific on anti-submarine and patrol operations.

PB4Y-1 LIBERATOR

67ft 3in.

17ft 11in.

110ft 0in.

A PB4Y-1 from the fifth batch of aircraft taken from the B-24D production line. It was delivered to the US Navy in January 1943 and assigned to Photo-Reconnaissance Squadron (VD) 1 before being transferred to VB-102. (72-AC-66A-77, RG72, NARA)

The first series of PB4Y-1s acquired by the US Navy had the glass nose of the standard B-24D, although it soon began modifying the aircraft with a nose extension to carry an ERCO bow turret. This PB4Y-1 is seen at Consolidated's plant in San Diego, California, in August 1943 after the completion of such a modification. (80G-70141, RG80, NARA)

Early PB4Y-1s were indistinguishable from the USAAF's B-24D, retaining the bomber's "glass" nose and armament of Browning M2 0.50-cal machine guns in a Martin top turret, Consolidated tail turret, Sperry belly turret, and two in the waist positions. The USAAF's standard olive drab over neutral gray camouflage scheme remained on the PB4Y-1s for months. With the 112th aircraft, the US Navy replaced the B-24D's glass nose with a revised front fuselage featuring an Engineering Research Corporation (ERCO) 250SH-3 bow turret.

ERCO had designed the turret for the PBB-1 Sea Ranger, but with the aircraft's cancelation it became available for the PB4Y-1. The ERCO turret had heavier armor protection for the gunner than comparable Consolidated and Emerson bow turrets, being fitted with a 1½-in. bullet-proof glass plate to protect the gunner's face, a ½-in. armor plate in front, and a ¼-in. armor plate in the floor. It also had a wider range of azimuth movement (right to left) and elevation (up and down) than the Consolidated and Emerson bow turrets. The gunner sat inside the turret, which contained 800 rounds of ammunition for the twin 0.50-cal machine guns. Early PB4Ys carried ASC and later ASG air-to-surface vessel (ASV) search radar. Later in 1944, the US Navy removed the Sperry belly turret on some PB4Y-1s and installed the improved AN/APS-15 search radar.

In 1943 the US Navy began working with Consolidated to develop an even more effective long-range land-based patrol bomber based on the PB4Y-1, and in May of that year it requested that Consolidated build three prototypes of the new aircraft, designated the PB4Y-2. It had a seven-foot fuselage extension added behind the flightdeck and a large single vertical stabilizer in place of the twin-tails on the PB4Y-1. Named Privateer, the PB4Y-2 had increased armament with, on the first 100 production aircraft, a Convair nose turret (later replaced with a ERCO bow turret) boasting twin 0.50-cal machine guns, two Martin dorsal turrets at the rear of the fuselage, two ERCO waist turrets with twin 0.50-cals, and a Motor Products Corporation (MPC) 250CH-6 tail turret. The PB4Y-2 was not fitted with the Sperry belly turret.

The Privateer was fitted with more powerful Pratt & Whitney R-1830-94 engines producing 1,350hp in revised nacelles in place of the PB4Y-1's Pratt & Whitney R-1830-65s. Since the PB4Ys rarely climbed to high altitudes during the course of their patrols, the US Navy removed the turbo-superchargers on the R-1830-94s so as to allow the PB4Y-2 to achieve higher speeds at lower altitudes. The fuselage extension on the PB4Y-2 enabled the Privateer to carry more radio, navigation, radar, and radar countermeasures (RCM) equipment. An additional radio/radar technician joined the crew.

The XPB4Y-2 first flew in September 1943 with the standard twin tail, but the second prototype changed to the single vertical stabilizer and began tests in February 1944. First deliveries to the US Navy began in March 1944. In January 1945 VPB-118 (all US Navy multi-engined VB squadrons having been re-designated VPB for Heavier-than-Air Patrol Bombing in October 1944) arrived on Tinian, in the Marianas, to begin operations. At the end of the war there were seven VPB squadrons equipped with the PB4Y-2 in the Pacific, with more units in the process of converting to the new patrol bomber. Production ended in October 1945 after the US Navy had received 739 PB4Y-2s.

The second PB4Y-2 prototype, BuNo 32096 spent much of its service career at the US Navy's test center at NAS Patuxent River. Initially built with a conventional Liberator twin tail, it was returned to Consolidated to be fitted with a single vertical tail following the completion of radio and radar equipment testing. BuNo 32096 was christened *Patuxent River Wart Hog* for all the bumps added to the lower fuselage to house electronic equipment. (80G-233033, RG80, NARA)

TECHNICAL
SPECIFICATIONS

TYPE 97 FLYING BOAT (H6K) "MAVIS"

The Type 97 Flying Boat Model 11 (H6K2) was the first production version of the "Mavis." Kawanishi initially completed ten of these aircraft, with an additional two built as staff transports and two more converted into transports as the H6K2-L for Dai Nippon Airways – a further 16 H6K2-Ls had been supplied to Dai Nippon by 1942.

The H6K2 was of all-metal construction with fabric-covered control surfaces. Four Mitsubishi Kinsei 43 14-cylinder air-cooled radial engines gave 1,000hp for take-off and 990hp at 3,940ft, the powerplants driving three-bladed metal propellers. The loaded weight of the H6K2 was 35,274lb, while the H6K2-L weighed slightly more at 37,699lb. At this weight, and with four 1,000hp engines, the H6K2 had a maximum speed of 206mph at 6,890ft and a cruising speed of 133mph, with a normal range of 2,479 miles. A crew of nine remained standard for all military models.

Before the start of the Pacific War, a detachment of H6Ks went to the Marshall Islands for operational training, which included clandestine photo-reconnaissance missions over the British Gilbert islands. Dai Nippon Airways used its transport models to fly a bi-weekly route from Yokohama to Palau via Saipan, which took around 15 hours in total. In January 1941 the airline began flying a new route from Palau to Jaluit, in the Marshall Islands, via Truk and Ponape, in the Caroline Islands.

The Type 97 Model 22 (H6K4) was the main production version, with Kawanishi completing 127 aircraft between 1939 and 1942. The company also built an additional

20 H6K4-L transports for the IJNAF. The flying boat was allocated the Allied reporting name "Mavis," as all Japanese bombers, reconnaissance aircraft, and flying boats received girls' names in the designation system devised by Capt Frank McCoy of the Material Section, Directorate of Intelligence, Allied Air Forces, Southwest Pacific Area in mid-1942. The H6K4 version had four Mitsubishi Kinsei 46 engines that produced 930hp for take-off and 1,070 hp at 13,780ft. The H6K4 could carry 2,950 imperial gallons of fuel, giving a maximum range of 3,779 miles and an airborne endurance of 26 hours.

The H6K4 was armed with one flexible 7.7mm Type 92 machine gun in an open bow position, another flexible 7.7mm weapon gun in an open dorsal position that replaced the earlier dorsal turret, two flexible 7.7mm machine guns in waist blisters just behind the wing, and a flexible 20mm Type 99 cannon in the tail turret, replacing the 7.7mm machine gun in the H6K2.

The H6K4's exceptional endurance made it ideal for long-range reconnaissance, although the lack of any self-sealing protection for the flying boat's fuel tanks meant the Type 97 was highly vulnerable when intercepted by Allied aircraft. Combats around Guadalcanal after the American landings on the island decimated the H6Ks of the Yokohama Kokutai. The Type 97 increasingly fell prey to Allied fighters and patrol aircraft, and by the end of 1942 the IJNAF steadily withdrew the "Mavis" from frontline flying boat units in favor of the H8K, although many remained on strength due to slow deliveries of its successor.

The Type 97 Transport Flying Boat Models 11 and 22 (H6K2-L and H6K4-L) had all military equipment removed and compartments installed for passengers and freight. The H6K2-L and H6K4-L built for Dai Nippon Airways contained a galley behind the flightdeck, a cabin which could seat eight in large, comfortable seats or four in fold-down beds, and a second cabin with single rows of five seats on either side of the fuselage. Separate compartments held freight and mail. The IJNAF's H6K2-Ls

An H6K4 carrying small 132lb bombs on a mounting attached to the underwing struts. During the early months of the war the IJN used the "Mavis" on several bombing missions. (2008-3-31_image_507_01, Peter M. Bowers Collection, MoF)

and H6K4-Ls served with transport units attached to its Koku Sentai (Air Flotilla) and Koko Kantai (Air Fleet).

The final production variant of the Type 97 was the Model 23 (H6K5), 36 examples of which were completed by Kawanishi during 1942. For the H6K5, the company replaced the Mitsubishi Kinsei 46 engines with more powerful Kinsei 53s, which produced 1,300hp for take-off and 1,200hp at 9,845ft. This change in powerplant increased the maximum speed to 239mph at 13,125ft and cruising speed to 161mph at the same altitude. Maximum range was slightly less than the H6K4. Armament was similar to the H6K4, with the exception of the machine gun in the open bow position which was replaced by a small turret just behind the flightdeck. The H6Ks all carried different types of radio for communications and for radio homing, with some H6K5s also being fitted with early ASV radar sets.

This remarkably close photograph of an "Emily" from the 851st Kokutai, taken on July 2, 1944 from an attacking PB4Y-1 of VB-115, shows the H8K's armament of dorsal, waist, and rear turret-mounted Type 99 20mm cannon. The weapon housed in the dorsal turret appears to be pointing away from the PB4Y-1, indicating that the Liberator gunners may have knocked it out of action. (80G-241258, RG80, NARA)

TYPE 2 FLYING BOAT (H8K) "EMILY"

The Model 11 (H8K1) was the first production version of the Type 2 Flying Boat. Kawanishi built three pre-production aircraft during 1941 and 12 full production flying boats in 1942. These incorporated modifications to the prototype to improve handling on water, as well as a slightly longer bow section, spray suppression strips, and a revised vertical tail. Mitsubishi MK4B Kasei 12 engines replaced the Kasei 11s used by the prototype. The H8K1 featured a revised armament compared to the 13-Shi prototype, with twin Type 92 7.7mm machine guns replacing the Type 99 20mm cannon in the bow turret and a Type 99 20mm cannon replacing the 7.7mm

H8K "EMILY" TAIL TURRET

1. Type 99 20mm fixed cannon
2. 45-, 60- or 100-round ammunition drum
3. Powered gun mount

4. Gun mount control pedals
5. Turret electrical connection box
6. Mounting for optical gunsight

7. Sliding turret doors
8. Gunner's seat
9. Protective armor plating

The transport versions of the Type 97 Flying Boat (H6K2-L/4-L) and the Type 2 Flying Boat (H8K2-L) Seiku performed a vital role for the IJN, particularly after the American advance across the Pacific cut off many of its island bases. Aircraft like the prototype of the H8K2-L Seiku, shown here, flew in supplies and evacuated key naval personnel. (2008-3-31_image_510_01, Peter M. Bowers Collection, MoF)

machine gun in the tail turret. Sliding hatches behind the pilot and co-pilot positions and underneath the wings had posts for mounting hand-held 7.7mm machine guns.

For reconnaissance missions, the H8K1's fuel tanks could hold 3,540 imperial gallons of fuel, giving this model a maximum range of 4,460 miles with an endurance of 24 hours. Assigned the Allied reporting name "Emily," the H8K1 normally carried a crew of nine or ten. Typically, the flying boat was manned by a nose observer and nose gunner/bombardier/navigator in the bow section, the pilot, co-pilot, and aircraft commander (who sat just behind the pilot), forward radio operator and engineer (who monitored the engines) in the spacious cockpit area ahead of the wing, the rear radio operator sat just aft of the dorsal turret, and the tail gunner occupying the tail turret beneath the rudder. The H8K often carried an additional passenger who would perform navigation, observation, or gunnery duties as needed. For the crew's comfort on long-range reconnaissance missions, the H8K had benches for relaxation and two beds so the crew could nap, an electric refrigerator and a toilet.

The Model 12 (H8K2) was the main production version of the Type 2 Flying Boat, with Kawanishi completing 111 aircraft during 1943–44 and a single example in 1945 when the focus shifted to building fighters. For the H8K2, Kawanishi changed to the more powerful Mitsubishi MK4Q Kasei 22 engine, which gave 1,850hp for take-off and 1,680hp at 6,890ft. This boosted the maximum speed to 290mph at 16,405ft, while maintaining the same cruising speed as the H8K1. The more powerful engines required more fuel, slightly reducing the normal maximum range of the H8K2. Empty weight increased to 40,521lb in part due to the provision of protection for the fuel tanks and crew.

Surprisingly for a Japanese aircraft at the time, but due to reports emanating from aerial combat in the Southwest Pacific, the IJNAF decided to protect the H8K's fuel tanks with gum rubber that swelled on contact with gasoline, sandwiched between two layers of hardened rubber inside the steel fuel tanks. An additional form of protection for the fuel tanks consisted of CO_2 bottles with lines to each fuel tank. The pilot could activate these bottles by means of a cable control placed just behind his seat, sending the CO_2 into a damaged fuel tank.

The H8K2 restored the Type 99 20mm cannon in the bow turret and, following combat experience with the H6K over the Solomons, added Type 99 20mm cannon in the two side blisters and a 20mm-thick steel plate behind the pilots' seats and behind the dorsal turret, which also had armor protection for the gunner. On late-production versions of the H8K2 sliding hatches replaced the glass side blisters. The bow and tail turrets both held five drums, each containing 45 rounds, for the 20mm nose cannon, while the dorsal turret had provision for ten drums of the same capacity. The hand-held 7.7mm machine gun stations had 12 drums, each containing 97 rounds.

The IJNAF added ASV radar to the H8K2, with its aerials fitted to either side of the fuselage behind the bow turret. When the H8K2 went into service it was the most well-armed and fastest flying boat fielded by any of the combatants in World War II.

The IJNAF requested Kawanishi modify the H8K into a transport flying boat to supplement the H6K2-L and H6K4-L. The company removed the fuel tanks from the lower hull and built a compartment extending from the bow to the rear step of the hull. It also installed a second compartment in the upper deck from behind the cockpit to the rear, removing the dorsal turret to make room for passengers and freight. Armament of the transport version consisted of a single Type 2 13mm machine gun in the bow turret and the Type 99 20mm cannon in the tail turret. The two compartments could hold 29 passengers or up to 64 troops on bench seats. Removing the fuselage fuel tanks reduced the transport's range to 2,750 miles.

The IJNAF accepted 36 aircraft as the Type 2 Transport Flying Boat Seiku (Clear Sky) Model 23 (H8K2-L). These served with the 1001st, 1021st, and 1081st Yuso Kokutai (Transport Air Group). As American forces advanced westward across the Pacific, the H8K2-Ls flew missions to isolated Japanese outposts to deliver supplies and evacuate key personnel. On one occasion transports from the 1081st Kokutai evacuated 600 men from Rabaul during a single nighttime operation.

PB4Y-1 LIBERATOR/PB4Y-2 PRIVATEER

The initial PB4Y-1 aircraft for the US Navy came directly from the USAAF's Consolidated B-24D production line with minimum modification (see *Osprey Duel 41 – B-24 Liberator vs Ki-43 "Oscar"* for a fuller description of the B-24D). The PB4Y-1 had four Pratt & Whitney R-1830-65 Twin Wasp engines in place of the B-24D's R-1830-43 engines, both versions providing 1,200hp for take-off and 1,100hp up to 25,000ft. The engine had a single-stage, single-speed, engine-driven supercharger, but for performance at altitude the B-24D had a General Electric B-2

A later model PB4Y-1, based on the USAAF's B-24J, from VD-5 undertakes a training mission over the USA in 1945. The US Navy acquired B-24D/J/L/Ms from Consolidated's vast production run, all of which were designated as PB4Y-1s. (80G-304015, RG80, NARA)

turbosupercharger installed behind each R-1830-43. Although the US Navy's PB4Y-1s flew their missions at lower altitudes, they retained the B-2 turbosuperchargers.

The B-24D had armament of a hand-held 0.50-cal Browning M2 machine gun in a mounting fixed in the front glazed nose, a Martin A-3 dorsal turret place behind the

The nose-mounted ERCO ball turret was the distinguishing feature of the PB4Y-1, and it equipped most PB4Y-2s as the ERCO 250SH-3. Designed for the Boeing PPB Sea Ranger flying boat, the ERCO 250SH-2/2A installed in the PB4Y-1 held 1,200 0.50-cal rounds within the turret structure and had a wider range of fire than comparable nose turrets. (80G-70144, RG80, NARA)

ERCO 250SH-2 BOW TURRET

1. 0.50-cal Browning M2 machine guns
2. Gun-charging handles
3. 0.50-cal ammunition
4. Link chutes
5. Ammunition tracks
6. Transparent ammunition track covers
7. Laminated bulletproof glass shield
8. N-9 reflector gunsight
9. Control handles with triggers
10. Gunner's arm rests
11. Gunner's seat
12. Front magazines
13. Side magazines
14. Headphone jack and radio controls
15. Seat adjustment lever

cockpit with twin 0.50-cals, a Consolidated A-6 turret with twin 0.50-cals in the tail and, on later models, a Sperry A-13 ball turret also with twin 0.50-cals. Finally, single 0.50-cals were installed in the two waist gun positions.

The US Navy retained this armament for the early B-24Ds transferred from the USAAF, although most PB4Y-1s were subsequently fitted with an ERCO bow turret in the nose with twin 0.50-cal M2 machine guns for added firepower. The PB4Y-1 had armor protection for the pilots and gunners, and self-sealing fuel tanks. Like the B-24D and later B-24J, M and L models, the PB4Y-1 could carry a large bombload of various weapons, such as eight 1,000lb bombs, up to 12 500lb or 250lb bombs and eight 325lb depth charges.

The later PB4Y-2 featured a heavier armament than the PB4Y-1. ERCO 250TH-1 self-contained tear drop turrets with twin 0.50-cal machine guns replaced the single 0.50-cal weapons in the open waist positions on the PB4Y-1. Like the ERCO ball turret, the magazines for the guns were located inside the tear drop turret. (NH-92482, NHHC)

On later PB4Y-1s, the US Navy replaced the Sperry ball turret with the AN/APS-15 ASV search radar (known as "George"), which a crewman lowered below the fuselage for operation. Extending the search radar reduced the bomber's speed by around 12mph. Normal maximum range on a patrol mission was 3,090 statute miles at a cruising speed of 149mph, and a bomb-bay fuel tank could extend the range to 3,440 miles – approximately 1,000 miles less than the Type 2 Flying Boat Model 12. This gave a normal search radius of 1,075 statute miles with a 20 percent fuel reserve. Carrying two 500lb bombs in addition to the bomb-bay tank reduced the range by 180 miles; not a significant loss. With the R-1830-65 engines, the PB4Y-1 had a maximum speed of 231mph at sea level under military power.

The PB4Y-2 Privateer was the result of the US Navy's effort to develop a dedicated, more capable land-based patrol aircraft that could replace both the Consolidated PB2Y flying boat and the PB4Y-1. In March 1943, the Bureau of Aeronautics ordered three XPB4Y-2 prototype aircraft from the company. The new patrol bomber would feature a lengthened fuselage, waist turrets, and an additional dorsal turret, more radar and electronic equipment, and new, more powerful Pratt & Whitney engines.

The first prototype flew in September 1943 with dummy turrets, and a second prototype, testing a lengthened fuselage, made its first flight at the end of October. The third prototype flew in December with the PB4Y-2's main recognition feature – a single vertical stabilizer that the USAAF had evaluated on the XB-24K from early September 1943. The single vertical stabilizer greatly improved the Liberator's flying characteristics, and while the single-tail B-24 did not go into production for the USAAF, the US Navy adopted the modification for the 660 PB4Y-2s it ordered in October 1943.

The US Navy removed the turbosuperchargers on the Pratt & Whitney R-1830-94 engines as they were unnecessary for low to medium altitude patrols. Their absence also provided a significant saving in weight. The new engines, with modified nacelles, gave the PB4Y-2 increased speed at sea level compared to the PB4Y-1 at a cost of slightly shorter range.

The most impressive change was to the PB4Y-2's armament. It featured five powered turrets, the heaviest armament of any US Navy patrol aircraft in World War II. These consisted of an ERCO 250SH-2/3 or Emerson 250CE-1 bow turret, two Martin 250CE upper deck turrets, two ERCO 250TH-1 self-contained tear drop turrets, one on either side of the fuselage, and a Consolidated 250CH or MPC 250CH-6 tail turret. Each turret contained twin 0.50-cal Browning M2 machine guns. The bow turret held 1,200 rounds, the tail turret and the two waist turrets 1,000 rounds each, and the two dorsal turrets 800 rounds apiece. The PB4Y-2 carried the same bomb load as the PB4Y-1. Early Privateers were fitted with the AN/APS-2F/G ASV radar, which was subsequently replaced with the later AN/APS-15B.

The Privateers began arriving in the Pacific in early 1945, and by the end of June the US Navy had seven PB4Y-2 and five PB4Y-1 squadrons in-theater, flying from airfields on Okinawa, in the Philippines, and on various smaller islands.

Comparison Specifications				
	Type 97 Model 22 H6K4	Type 2 Model 12 H8K2	PB4Y-1 Liberator	PB4Y2 Privateer
Number built	215	167	977	792
Powerplant	4 x 1,000hp Mitsubishi Kinsei 43	4 x 1,850hp Mitsubishi Kasei 22	4 x 1,200hp Pratt & Whitney R-1830-65	4 x 1,350hp Pratt & Whitney R-1830-94
Dimensions				
Span	131ft 2in.	124ft 8in.	110ft	110ft
Length	84ft	92ft 3in.	67ft 3in.	74ft 7in.
Height	20ft 6in.	30ft	17ft 11in.	30ft 1in.
Weights				
Empty	25,810lb	40,521lb	36,950lb	37,485lb
Loaded	47,399lb	71,650lb	60,000lb	65,000lb
Performance				
Max speed	211mph at 13,125ft	290mph at 16,405ft	223mph at sea level	237mph at 13,750ft
Cruising speed	146mph at 6,550ft	184mph at 13,125ft	148mph at 1,500ft	195mph at 10,000ft
Max range	3,779 miles	4,445 miles	2,960 miles	2,880 miles
Armament	3 x Type 92 7.7mm machine guns 1 x Type 99 20mm cannon	5 x Type 92 7.7mm machine guns 5 x Type 99 20mm cannon	10 x 0.50-cal Browning M2 machine guns	12 x 0.50-cal Browning M2 machine guns

THE STRATEGIC SITUATION

The first combat between a US Navy PB4Y-1 Liberator and an IJNAF flying boat did not take place until August 1943, 18 months after the beginning of the Pacific War. By this point in the conflict, having failed to dislodge Allied troops on New Guinea and Guadalcanal and having suffered the loss of much of its carrier fleet, the Japanese were on the defensive. Momentum was moving inexorably toward the Allies, who would increasingly dictate the war's pace and direction. Aerial combat between rival maritime patrol aircraft over the following 18 months would reflect the progressive westward progress of American forces across the central Pacific under Adm Chester Nimitz, Allied ground and air units under Gen Douglas MacArthur in New Guinea, and under Adm William Halsey up the Solomon Islands chain to the Bismarck Archipelago.

Japan's rationale for going to war, and its primary objective, was to seize the resources the Japanese leadership believed were essential for the country's survival, especially oil from the Dutch East Indies. In a lightning campaign, Japan conquered all of Southeast Asia, captured the Gilbert Islands in Micronesia, the main islands in the Bismarck Archipelago, and established footholds in the Solomon Islands and New Guinea. Having obtained their objectives, the Japanese military now had to secure and maintain them against the inevitable Allied response.

Japan's strategy had been to create a defensive barrier and wage a defensive war, inflicting such losses on the Allies that their will to continue the conflict would steadily erode, leaving Japan in command of what it called the Greater East Asia Co-Prosperity Sphere. The area that Japan now had to defend stretched from the Kurile Islands north

A news photograph of H6Ks undergoing maintenance at a base somewhere in the South Pacific. Several of the mechanics have stripped down to cope with the intense heat. (Author's Collection)

of Japan, to the Gilbert Islands in the Pacific, New Guinea and the Solomons, Burma in the west, and all of China and Manchuria. Defending an area of this size was well beyond the military and economic resources that Japan had available.

Nevertheless, during 1942 the Japanese made every effort to retain the strategic initiative, launching carrier strikes in the Indian Ocean, attempting an advance in New Guinea, deepening its hold on the Solomon Islands and seeking a decisive battle with the American aircraft carriers at Midway. This simultaneous pursuit of multiple objectives only served to dissipate Japan's efforts with little positive result.

In the aerial battles over the Solomon Islands the IJNAF suffered severe losses of experienced pilots and aircrews. Adm Isoroku Yamamoto's Operation *I-Go* air offensive launched on April 1, 1943, which was intended to severely damage advanced Allied positions in New Guinea and the Solomons and thereby protect the Japanese barrier, ended in failure.

In June the Allies launched Operation *Cartwheel*, intended to neutralize the Japanese base at Rabaul on New Britain in the Bismarck Archipelago. While Gen MacArthur's American and Australian forces seized control of the northeastern coast of New Guinea, Adm Halsey's forces moved up the Solomon Islands chain, landing on Bougainville on November 1, 1943. A second Japanese air offensive, Operation *RO*, launched from Rabaul in November 1943, also failed with significant losses.

That same month Adm Nimitz began his campaign in the Central Pacific with the capture of Tarawa and Makin Atoll in the Gilbert Islands. This two-pronged advance against the Japanese to break through the defensive barrier and reach the home islands was the basis of Allied strategy for defeating Japan in the Pacific.

Allied grand strategy had as its primary objective the defeat of Germany. This "Germany First" strategy placed priority on the allocation of resources to the Allied forces fighting in Europe – and adopting a defensive strategy against Japan in the

An H8K rests on beaching gear next to a Nakajima A6M2-N Navy Type 2 Floatplane Fighter on an island somewhere in the Pacific. (80G-214899, RG80, NARA)

Pacific. Following Allied efforts to halt a Japanese advance toward Australia with countermoves in New Guinea and the landings and defense of Guadalcanal, in early 1943 at the Casablanca Conference, the combined American and British chiefs of staff agreed on the continuation of an offensive in New Guinea and the Solomons to neutralize the Japanese position on Rabaul, and an advance in the Central Pacific. The latter had long been a key aspect of the US Navy's planning for a war against Japan under War Plan Orange.

At the Trident Conference in May, the Allies agreed to an expanded offensive in the Central Pacific to capture positions in the Gilbert Islands (Operation *Galvanic*) and then push on to the Marshall Islands (Operations *Flintlock* and *Catchpole*). Later, at the Quadrant Conference in August, the Combined Chiefs of Staff approved a plan for Nimitz's Central Pacific forces to advance beyond the Marshall Islands to capture positions in the Marianas (Operation *Forager*) and the Palaus (Operation *Stalemate*) in 1944, while MacArthur's forces moved progressively west along the New Guinea coast and Halsey's forces captured islands in the Bismarcks to complete the isolation of Rabaul.

The longer term objective was to recapture the Philippines, MacArthur's preferred objective, or to seize positions on Formosa (as Taiwan was then called) or on the coast of China to serve as a base for an invasion of Japan. An intense debate between the US Army and the US Navy on objectives and the correct strategy for the defeat of Japan would prompt America's war industry to increase production to provide sufficient resources to continue the two-pronged advance across the Pacific. This would lead to the capture of the Marianas in the summer of 1944, MacArthur's invasion of the Philippines in October 1944, and the continuation of the island advance toward Japan with the invasion of Iwo Jima in February 1945 and Okinawa two months later.

The success of the Allied advances in the South and Southwest Pacific, and the American advance across the Central Pacific, was heavily dependent on Allied land-based and carrier-based air power. In a war of attrition, destroying enemy forces and equipment, by any means, was a key to victory. The destruction of Japanese supplies through air and submarine attacks on lines of communications, particularly the sinking of Japanese merchant vessels, wearing down Japanese air power to provide greater freedom for Allied bombing attacks, and attacks on Japanese bases all helped stretch Japan's over-burdened logistical system to breaking point.

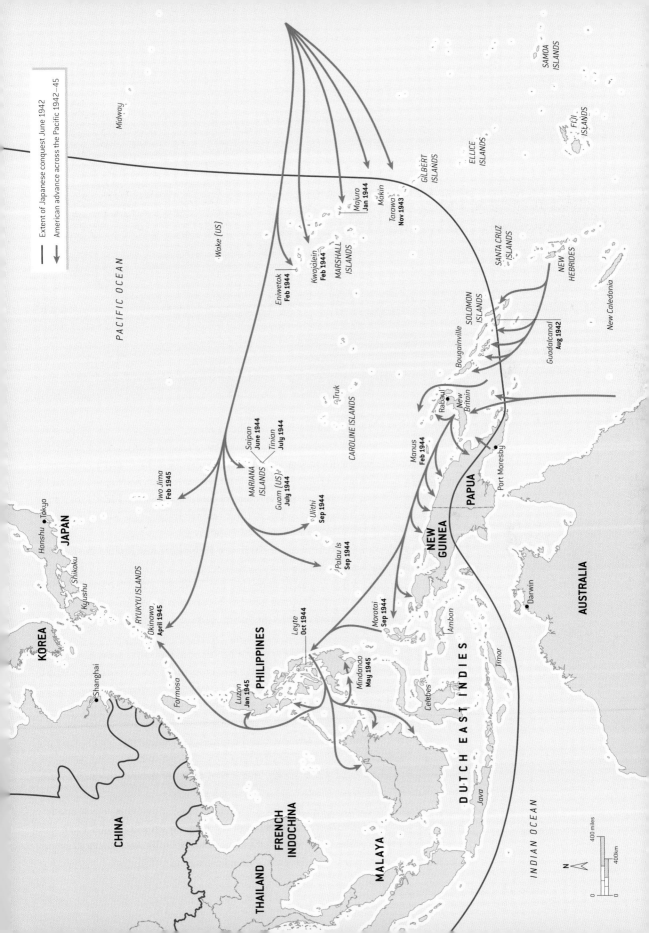

Extent of Japanese conquest June 1942

American advance across the Pacific 1942–45

PACIFIC OCEAN

Midway

Wake [US]

SAMOA ISLANDS

FIJI ISLANDS

ELLICE ISLANDS

GILBERT ISLANDS

Makin

Tarawa
Nov 1943

Majuro
Jan 1944

Kwajalein
Feb 1944

MARSHALL ISLANDS

Eniwetok
Feb 1944

SANTA CRUZ ISLANDS

NEW HEBRIDES

New Caledonia

SOLOMON ISLANDS

Bougainville

Guadalcanal
Aug 1942

Truk

CAROLINE ISLANDS

Ulithi

Palau Is
Sep 1944

Guam [US]
July 1944

MARIANA ISLANDS

Saipan
June 1944

Tinian
July 1944

Iwo Jima
Feb 1945

Rabaul

New Britain

Manus
Feb 1944

Port Moresby

PAPUA

NEW GUINEA

JAPAN

Honshu

Tokyo

Shikoku

Kyushu

RYUKYU ISLANDS

Okinawa,
April 1945

KOREA

Shanghai

Formosa

PHILIPPINES

Luzon
Jan 1945

Leyte
Oct 1944

Mindanao
May 1945

Morotai
Sep 1944

Ambon

Celebes

Timor

Darwin

AUSTRALIA

DUTCH EAST INDIES

Java

INDIAN OCEAN

CHINA

THAILAND

FRENCH INDOCHINA

MALAYA

N

0   400 miles
0   400km

The IJN, like the US Navy, relied on seaplane tenders to service its flying boats where there were no land bases. Here, the crew of the seaplane tender *Akitsushima II* practice loading an H8K from the 802nd Kokutai in the early summer of 1942. The vessel was sunk by carrier aircraft from the US Navy's Task Force 58 in Coron Bay, in the western Philippines, on September 24, 1944. (PG051648, Kure Maritime Museum)

One of the key contributing factors to Allied victory over Japan was the impressive ability of US Army and US Navy engineer and construction battalions to carve out airstrips from the jungle or on coral islands in a short space of time. Just as important was the US Navy's highly effective supply chain, which connected the west coast of America with the far reaches of the Pacific to sustain the immense Fast Carrier Task Force and its various island bases. In each theater, newly captured islands served as stepping stones for the next operation.

These jungle and island airfields in the South and Southwest Pacific, the Central Pacific islands, and later in the Philippines were home to land-based PB4Y Liberator and PV Ventura/Harpoon patrol aircraft that served along with PBY Catalina and Martin PBM Mariner flying boats in the US Navy's patrol squadrons. The PB4Y squadrons followed the advance across the Pacific, leap-frogging from one island chain to another.

Operating from bases in the Phoenix and Ellis Islands, the PB4Ys scouted Japanese bases in the Gilberts; moving to the Gilbert Islands after their capture, the PB4Y squadrons supported the advance to the Marshalls, and from there to the Marianas. Similarly, PB4Y squadrons began operations from Guadalcanal and moved with the advance to bases in the Admiralty Islands and along the northern coast of New Guinea to Morotai, in the Halmahera Islands, and then on to the Philippines. From bases on Tinian, in the Marianas, and then on Iwo Jima, the PB4Y squadrons could patrol the sea routes to Japan, and from bases on Okinawa the sea approaches to the Japanese home islands themselves.

The primary mission of all US Navy patrol aircraft was reconnaissance. Constant patrolling was vital to locating units of the Japanese fleet, the status of forces on Japan's island bases, and to protecting the US Navy's own lines of communications. This was especially true during the approach and initial stages of invasions, when supporting

Two PB4Y-1s head out on a patrol from their base on Kwajalein in March 1944. The lead aircraft carries ASV radar antennas under both wings. As American forces advanced west across the Pacific, the patrol bomber squadrons followed in their wake as soon as US Army and US Navy construction battalions had completed the building of airfields on the newly captured islands. (80G-407717, RG80, NARA)

forces would be vulnerable to attack. As the advance in the Central Pacific continued westward, there was a need to monitor bypassed Japanese bases in the Gilberts, Marshall, and Caroline Islands.

Operating from island bases, the patrol aircraft would typically fly fan-shaped sectors covering the most critical approaches, with the flying boats and their seaplane tenders providing coverage until airfields could be built for the land-based PB4Ys and PVs. Having fast, heavily armed land-based patrol aircraft capable of carrying a useful load of bombs enabled the US Navy to employ new offensive tactics for its patrol aircraft. If it did not interfere with the primary mission, the US Navy encouraged the patrol squadrons to go after targets of opportunity and to make raids on bypassed Japanese installations.

Reconnaissance was even more vital to the IJN. To defend the far-flung outposts along its defensive barrier, the IJN had to know when and where American forces might strike. While the IJN broadly knew the route an American fleet was likely to take across the Pacific, determining the exact location of an advancing force and its probable target were key factors in deciding where to move units to provide the best possible defense. The difficulty the IJNAF faced was the lack of long-range reconnaissance aircraft in adequate numbers to cover the broad expanse of the Pacific, as well as a lack of attention to developing effective methods and doctrine for long-range reconnaissance missions.

In late 1942 the IJNAF reorganized its flying boat force in the Pacific into three Kokutai – the 801st, 802nd, and 851st. By early 1944 these units covered a wide arc from Japan to Southeast Asia. The 801st Kokutai was assigned to the 27th Koku Sentai (part of the 12th Koku Kantai), sending its aircraft from Japan on operations over the Pacific, covering the area from Japan to Saipan. The 802nd Kokutai was based at Truk as part of the 22nd Koku Sentai in the 14th Koku Kantai, patrolling the

By September 1944, the US Navy had moved VB-102 and VB-116 to Tinian, extending the range of Liberator patrols closer to Japan. These two PB4Y-1s of VB-102, now in the US Navy's three-tone camouflage scheme, were photographed between missions at the airfield on Tinian. Like their USAAF counterparts, the men flying the PB4Y found the aircraft's slab-sided fuselage an excellent "canvas" for nose art. (San Diego Air and Space Museum Collection)

Caroline and Marshall Islands area, while the 851st Kokutai was assigned to the 28th Koku Sentai in the 13th Koku Kantai based in Sumatra, covering the Indian Ocean and Dutch East Indies area, but also regularly flying operations between the Philippines and the Marianas. By the middle of 1943, the main equipment of the three flying boat units was the H8K2, but each unit rarely had more than 12 aircraft on hand. The Kokutai also had, in addition, a few H6K2/4s.

The flying boat Kokutai classified aircrew as those who could perform any type of mission, those capable of daylight missions only and beginners new to operations. A lack of aircrew meant that many had to fly beyond the point of efficiency. This was detrimental to performance of the flying boat units, as the IJNAF's obsession with attack had already led it to neglect training for reconnaissance crews.

In the first part of the war, IJNAF flying boats conducted offensive operations, bombing targets in Australia and as far afield as Calcutta, in India, Trincomalee, in Ceylon (present day Sri Lanka), and Canton Island, in the South Pacific. As the war intensified, and the risk of running into Allied aircraft became more commonplace with expanded radar coverage, H6K/H8K losses increased to the point where the flying boat units had to abandon offensive operations in order to concentrate on long-range reconnaissance. They were also tasked with flying to bypassed islands to deliver supplies and evacuate stranded aircrew and maintenance personnel initially by day but increasingly by night and in poor weather to avoid interception.

As the US Navy sent more PB4Y squadrons to the Central and Southwest Pacific, the IJNAF flying boats had more encounters with US Navy Liberators. It was standard procedure for a flying boat to send out a contact report when the crew had sighted an enemy aircraft, but frequently there would be no signal and no return of the aircraft from a patrol. It is astonishing that there were any contacts between patrolling Japanese flying boats and PB4Ys, given the immensity of the Pacific Ocean area, but both navies flew missions in the same areas, and the US Navy had a singular advantage. Having broken the IJN's code system, it knew not only the locations and strength of the Japanese "Emily" and "Mavis" units, but the times of departure of the flying boat transport runs from Japan to Truk and Palau, and from Truk to Rabaul.

THE COMBATANTS

US NAVY AIRCREW TRAINING

PB4Y-1 crews typically consisted of 11 men, made up of three officers and eight enlisted personnel. The nucleus of the crew was the Patrol Plane Commander (PPC), two co-pilots, the Plane Captain and his assistant, two radio men, an ordnance man, and three gunners. The PPC was the senior pilot, usually a lieutenant with previous combat experience, often a tour with a PBY Catalina squadron. Two junior co-pilots relieved the pilot on long patrol missions, with one co-pilot acting as navigator. As the US Navy expanded its PB4Y squadrons, a shortage of pilots led to assigning full time navigators who had no flight training but who had completed intensive training in navigation. The co-pilots also had training in gunnery and could relieve gunners if needed.

The Plane Captain was the senior enlisted man on the crew, usually an Aviation Machinists Mate (AMM) Chief or 1st Class, and he served as the flight engineer on the aircraft. He had responsibility for all the enlisted crewmen and all pre-flight checks, with a second AAM as his assistant; both also served as gunners. The crew contained two radio operators, the first and second Aviation Radioman (ARM), who alternated between operating the radios, managing all communications and manning the top dorsal turret. An Aviation Ordnanceman (AOM) was responsible for checking each gun position and supervising the loading of bombs before each flight, serving as a gunner once aloft. In some crews an ordnance man would also perform the role of bombardier. Three dedicated gunners, who manned one of the waist gun positions, the belly turret and the tail turret completed the crew. Every member of the crew had undergone intensive training in his specialty.

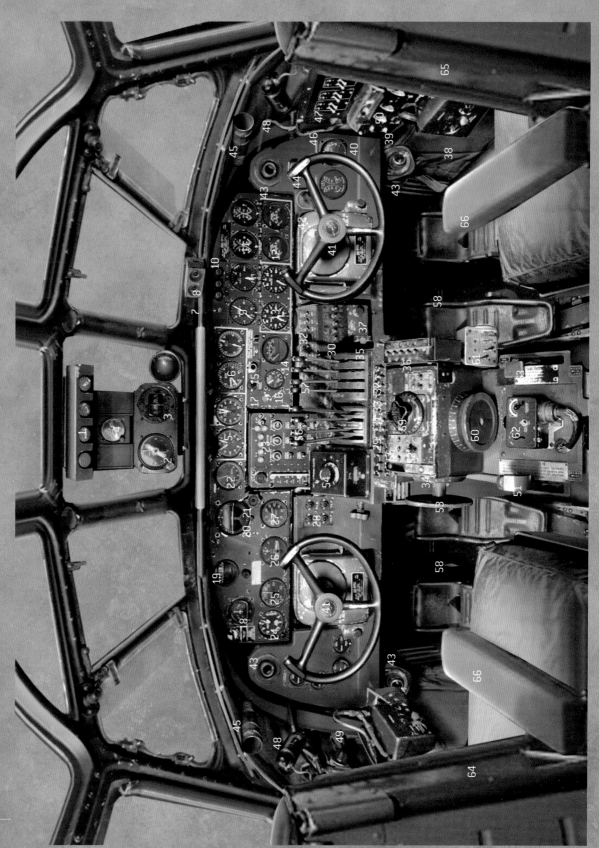

PPCs were often graduates of the US Navy's pre-war training program at Naval Air Station (NAS) Pensacola, Florida. Before the war the US Navy had established the V-5 program for prospective Naval Aviators who, if they successfully completed flight training, would receive commissions as Ensigns in the US Naval Reserve or as 2nd Lieutenants in the US Marine Corps Reserve. After passing a physical exam, the prospective cadet went to one of 16 Naval Reserve Aviation Bases around the country for elimination training. This 30-day course gave cadets ten hours of dual flying instruction and an introduction to ground school courses. If successful, the cadet went on to Pensacola, the home of Naval Aviation, for flight training, beginning with six weeks of ground instruction and physical training.

Ground instruction covered such topics as aircraft powerplants and structures, theory of flight, gunnery, navigation, aerology, and communications. After six weeks the cadet began flight training while continuing ground instruction for an additional nine weeks, alternating flying with classroom work. Squadron 1 covered primary training, where the cadet practiced basic maneuvers, take-offs and landings, formation and night flying on the Navy N3N (nicknamed the "Yellow Peril" because of its color), both land and float versions, or Stearman N2S biplane trainers. If successful, the cadet progressed to Squadron 2, where he flew heavier aircraft. In the pre-war period these were often second-line US Navy biplanes like the Vought O3U, but the North American NJ-1 with fixed landing gear and the SNJ with retractable landing gear were acquired from the late 1930s. Squadron 3 taught instrument flying in the Link Trainer and in a training aircraft, where the cadet flew "under the hood."

Having completed basic training, the cadet then moved to advanced training in the type of aircraft he would fly in service. A prospective flying boat pilot joined Squadron 5, where he would be introduced to large, twin-engined flying boats, flying the older Consolidated P2Y or Martin P3M, and then the PBY. After receiving his commission, the new Ensign would join a regular patrol squadron, where he would serve as a junior pilot and continue his training to become fully qualified.

After President Franklin D. Roosevelt called for a huge expansion in the number of aircraft flown by the USAAC and the US Navy in the late 1930s, the Civilian Pilot

1. Propeller feathering switches	21. Gyro horizon control knob	37. Defroster control	54. Turbo boost selector
2. Remote indicating compass	22. Radio compass bearing	38. Co-pilot's oxygen panel	55. Wing running light switches
3. Magnetic compass	indicator	39. Ignition switches	56. Throttles
4. Clock	23. C-1 automatic pilot	40. Switch guard	57. Mixture control
5. Manifold pressure gauges	24. Altimeter	41. Pilot and co-pilot's yokes	58. Rudder pedals
6. Tachometers	25. Airspeed indicator	42. Formation light rheostat	59. Rudder tabs control knob
7. Bomb-bay doors indicator	26. Turn-and-bank indicator	43. Ventilators	60. Aileron control wheel
8. Bomb release indicator	27. Rate-of-climb indicator	44. Defroster duct	61. Recognition light switches
9. Fuel pressure gauges	28. Propeller governor limit	45. Master heater vents	62. Command radio transmitter
10. Supercharger warning plate	lights	46. Main storage battery	control box
11. Cylinder temperature gauges	29. Bomb-bay fuel transfer	switches	63. Wing flap control lever
12. Oil temperature gauges	switches	47. Defroster fan switches	64. Pilot's seat
13. Oil pressure gauges	30. Engine starter switches	48. 24-volt D.C. fluorescent	65. Co-pilot's seat
14. Free air temperature gauge	31. Booster pump switches	lights	66. Arm rests
15. Landing gear indicator light	32. Oil dilution switches	49. Fluorescent light switch	
16. Flap position indicator	33. Primer switches	50. Emergency ignition switch	
17. Marker beacon indicator	34. SCR 595 IFF power switch	bar	
18. Pilot direction indicator	35. SCR 595 IFF emergency	51. Landing gear control lever	
19. Directional gyro	switch	52. Alarm button	
20. Gyro horizon	36. De-icer control	53. Elevator control wheel	

Many patrol bomber pilots who went through their training before the start of the Pacific War received instruction on older US Navy flying boats retired from frontline service before learning to fly the PBY. Here, student pilots at NAS Pensacola board a P2Y prior to conducting a training flight in April 1940. (80G-464611, RG80, NARA)

Training Program (CPTP) became an important source of aviation cadets for both services. This program provided college students with 35 to 40 hours of flight instruction in light aircraft and 72 hours of ground school, and while there was no requirement to join the military, most graduates of the program went into the USAAC or US Navy aviation training programs. After the outbreak of war, the CPTP became the War Training Service, and it saved both USAAC/USAAF and the US Navy considerable time by eliminating those unfit for flying and giving primary instruction to those who were successful.

During 1942 the US Navy revised and standardized its flight training program to produce the thousands of pilots that were now needed more efficiently. On joining the Naval Aviation training program, cadets began with 15 weeks of ground instruction at a flight preparatory school, moving on to three months of primary flight training at one of the War Training Service schools. If successful, the cadet was sent to one of the US Navy's new pre-flight schools for 11 weeks of ground instruction and physical training. Once this had been completed, the aviation cadet was then ready for primary training at one of 15 primary training bases the US Navy set up across the country. At these schools the cadets went through six stages of flight training over 12 weeks, still on the N3N and N2S biplane trainers, gaining the skills of precision flying by day and by night.

From there, the cadet went on to intermediate training at Pensacola or a large new training facility the US Navy established at NAS Corpus Christi, Texas. Here, the cadet spent four weeks on basic training in Vultee SNV monoplane trainers, moving on to instrument flying and more intermediate training in the SNJ. During intermediate training the US Navy assigned cadets to the type of aircraft he would fly in service, based on personal preference, skill levels, and its requirements. Cadets selected for patrol aircraft initially trained on the PBY, but later in the war the US Navy acquired the twin-engined Beech SNB to teach cadets the fundamentals of flying multi-engined aircraft prior to moving on to the PBY.

Aircrewmen in the US Navy performed two tasks on naval aircraft: serving as technicians with specialized skills – aircraft mechanics, radio and communications, and ordnance – and as gunners. Training men to become aircrew took around nine months.

As the war progressed, the US Navy began specialized training for bombardiers using the twin-engined Beech SNB, shown here on a training mission out of NAS Jacksonville, Florida, in March 1943. With a growing number of land-based patrol aircraft, the US Navy also used the SNB in place of the older PBY to introduce students to multi-engined aircraft. (80G-407294, RG80, NARA)

The enlisted man began his service with six to eight weeks of training at a boot camp, where he received intensive training in US Navy rules and regulations and physical conditioning. After completing boot camp, a Seaman who had scored highly on aptitude tests would be assigned to a technical training school for four-and-a-half months of tuition in a specialty.

The US Navy established a large "Class A" technical training center in Norman, Oklahoma, to train aviation mechanics, ordnance men, and maintenance personnel. One of the largest schools at Norman was for Aviation Mechanics, who went through four phases of training to learn how to maintain aircraft and engines. AOM trained in all aspects of naval aerial weapons, covering machine guns and cannon, turrets and their gunsights, and bombs and torpedoes, learning how to prepare them for combat operations; they trained in operational aircraft during this phase of the course. ARM trained in Morse code to be able to receive 16–18 words per minute and in operating aircraft radio equipment, and as the war went on, radar and RCM sets too. Bombardiers, both officers and enlisted men, took a three-month course in aerial bombing using SNBs and PBYs as well as synthetic training devices. All aircrewmen went through a five-week gunnery training course.

Aircrew came together at operational training units. To relieve frontline squadrons from the burden of training new pilots and aircrew to operational standards, the US

After completing their training or preparing for a second combat tour, Naval Aviators transitioned to the PB4Y at the operational training unit at NAS Jacksonville, and later in the war at NAS Hutchinson, Kansas. During operational training the US Navy grouped officers and enlisted men into crews that would fly together in combat.
(80G-414394, RG80, NARA)

Navy set up operational training units to provide specialized tuition in combat tactics. Operational training on the PB4Y started at NAS Jacksonville, Florida, but shifted to NAS Hutchinson, Kansas, in 1944. For pilots, the two-month operational training course began with familiarization on the PB4Y. For experienced pilots, this would be conversion from another aircraft type, while for newly graduated Ensigns the objective was to produce a fully trained first pilot, the first step on the way to becoming a PPC. During operational training a pilot would record around 100 hours of flying time.

Training for land-based patrol bombers stressed instrument and night flying, navigation, search and attack tactics, including horizontal and glide bombing, and gunnery. Enlisted men received tuition in their respective specialties from qualified instructors, and they were also given more gunnery training. During operational training, the US Navy assigned pilots and enlisted men to a crew who duly combined their training on practice patrol missions that integrated all their skills to build an effective combat team. Having completed the two-month operational training program, the entire crew would then join a PB4Y squadron assigned to the Atlantic or Pacific Fleet.

US NAVY AERIAL GUNNERY TRAINING

Before receiving his air gunner's insignia after completing the five-week course in air gunnery, a new gunner swore the following oath:

> I am a United States Naval Aircrewman, member of a combat team. My pilot and shipmates place their trust in me and my guns. I will care for my plane and guns as I care for my life. In them I hold the power of life and death – life for my countrymen, death for the enemy. I will uphold my trust by protecting my pilot and plane to the absolute limit of my ability.

US Navy gunnery training combined theory and practice. Prospective gunners first learned how to operate and maintain the 0.30-cal and 0.50-cal machine guns until stripping, cleaning, installing, and arming the weapons became second nature. Instruction placed a heavy emphasis on correcting malfunctions, learning what caused the problem, and how to rapidly fix it. The same effort went into learning the different gunsights and how to use them, and the several types of turret installed in US Navy

aircraft. Hours went into aircraft recognition until the student could identify the ten principal types of USAAF, US Navy, British, German, and Japanese aircraft.

Gunnery practice commenced with the shotgun, shooting clay pigeons to begin training the eye for deflection shooting. The next stage introduced students to machine guns, and they initially fired at fixed targets, before progressing to moving targets whilst sat in an actual gun turret. The targets either moved around on a track in front of a fixed turret, or the turrets were mounted on a moving truck and the gunner shot at fixed targets. At some gunnery schools, trainee gunners did air-to-air firing from the back seat of an SNJ, targeting a towed sleeve, while at other facilities the trainees would fire at towed sleeves from turrets on the ground. Gunnery training continued once the new gunner joined an operational training unit.

The US Navy began the war teaching gunners the "2/3 method," where the gunner calculated the lead angle (the distance ahead of the attacking or attacked aircraft) in mils, or rings on the gunsight, based on the speed of the target, with the lead calculated as two-thirds of the target aircraft's speed. Later, the US Navy adopted what it called the "position firing method" (which had been proven in combat as being the best way of shooting down attacking fighters) when training its gunners in deflection shooting.

The position firing method taught how to fire at fighters as they entered into a pursuit curve. It recognized that in order to hit the aircraft under attack, the enemy fighter had to maintain the curve of pursuit to register hits. The correct lead and aiming point the gunner needed to employ in order to hit an attacking fighter could be mathematically computed using the radius of the gunner's ring or reflecting sight and the distance from the center of the sight to its inner and two outer rings, known as "rads," to calculate the correct deflection. The method envisioned the fighter's attack profile as a series of four cones spreading out from behind, ahead, or directly above and below the bomber. The numbers of the cones – 1/2, 1, 2, and 3 – gave the gunner

PB4Y gunners went through intensive gunnery tuition, beginning with skeet shooting and continuing on with training in the turrets they would man in combat. Other crewmen went through a shorter course so that gunnery duties could be rotated during a patrol mission and the gun positions manned at all times. Here, gunnery students fire 0.30-cal M2/AN machine guns in makeshift turrets during training in March 1944. (80G-473843, RG80, NARA)

the number of rads, or deflection, to allow when aiming at the oncoming fighter depending on its distance and angle of approach. Mastering the position firing method took hours of practice.

IJNAF AIRCREW TRAINING

IJNAF student pilots selected to fly floatplanes and flying boats trained on the Yokosuka Type 90 Training Seaplane K4Y1, then moved to the floatplane version of the Yokosuka Navy Type 93 Intermediate Trainer K5Y2. Here, a young trainee stands proudly on the port float of a K5Y2. (Author's Collection)

IJNAF aircrew training was intensive and highly selective, with only a small proportion of potential pilots completing flight training pre-war. The IJNAF made the decision to rely on an elite corps of exceptional pilots, which proved adequate for the short, victorious campaign in the early months of the Pacific War. However, this proved to be a fatal error in judgement once Japan entered a war of attrition with the United States.

The IJNAF drew its pilots and aircrew from the small number of graduates at the Naval Academy at Etajima island, in Hiroshima Bay, from men serving in the IJN, the small Koku Yobi Gakusei (Air Reserve Student) Program that drew from universities, and from the Hiko Yoka Renshu (Flight Reserve) Program, which recruited boys from the age of 15 who had completed several years of middle school. Those selected duly completed a three-year training program, with the third year featuring intensive training in aviation subjects. These pilots were known as Yokoren. This program produced the enlisted pilots who formed the bulk of the IJNAF's pilot and aircrew cadre.

Flying training comprised three phases: primary, intermediate, and operational. Prior to the attack on America, the primary and advanced training programs took around 12 months to complete. Training took place at the IJN base at Kasumigaura, northeast of Tokyo near Japan's second largest lake, and at several other sites around Japan. Kasumigaura was, for IJNAF pilots, the equivalent of Pensacola in the US Navy. All trainees went through the same primary training course flying the Yokosuka Type 90 K4Y1 primary training aircraft. After three months of training in basic flying

飛沫ヲ揚ゲテ（適性飛行）　土浦海軍航空隊

横鎮第二七號ノ一〇四ノ二　昭和十七年十月九日許可濟

skills, and having soloed, the IJNAF divided the trainees into groups, who would go on to fly carrier aircraft, land-based aircraft, floatplanes, and flying boats.

Those trainees selected for floatplanes and flying boats began on the Yokosuka Type 90 Seaplane Trainer, a twin-float version of the Type 90 primary training aircraft developed during the 1930s but still in use at the beginning of the war. Trainee pilots would progress to the Yokosuka Type 93 Intermediate Trainer K5Y2. The latter, used to train prospective floatplane and flying boat pilots on Lake Kasumigaura, also featured twin floats. Because of its yellow-orange paint scheme, IJNAF pilots dubbed the K5Y2 the akatombo (red dragonfly). Trainee pilots learned more advanced flying techniques, including aerobatics and cross-country navigation, in the K5Y2.

After completing their intermediate training course in nine to ten months and gaining their wings, the new pilots moved on to an operational training unit that specialized in the type of aircraft they would fly in combat, usually at an airfield in Japan. At these units the pilots would be instructed in how to fly operational aircraft, typically older models that the IJNAF had withdrawn from frontline service, and they would practice the techniques subsequently used by them in combat.

While flying boat pilots in the pre-war period may have received training on the older Navy Type 15 Flying Boat (H1H1) and Type 89 Flying Boat (H2H1), many went from the K5Y2 to the twin-engined Yokosuka H5Y1 Type 99 Medium Flying Boat. Having proved unsuccessful in its intended role as a complement to the larger H6K, the H5Y1 (only 20 of which were built) became an operational training aircraft for flying boat pilots. Later in the war the Aichi Kokuki K.K. built 24 small twin-engined Type 2 Training Flying Boat Model 11s (H9As) to train flying boat pilots.

This pre-war tinted Japanese postcard shows trainees taking off from Lake Kasumigaura, the home of IJNAF flight training, in their Type 93 Intermediate Trainers. (Author's Collection)

During the war, the transition from the H6K to the H8K was often done "on the job," with pilots receiving only a week of training before taking control of a Type 2, having had no training in night flying. Such a switch was made possible because the pre-war pilots trained to fly the H6K were exceptionally well-qualified, with extensive tuition in celestial navigation.

The biggest problem encountered by pilots transitioning from the H6K to the H8K was the difference in height between the cockpits of the two flying boats, and the drastically altered perspective this created. Pilots flying the H6K enjoyed a view of the horizon out of the cockpit window, giving them an intuitive sense of the proper attitude for landing and take-off. This was totally lost with the larger H8K, as its cockpit was positioned considerably higher. Pilots accustomed to the H6K would often find that they pulled the nose of the H8K too high above the horizon out of habit, leading to porpoising. Following fixes to this problem (explained earlier in this volume) and more flying training, the porpoising issue disappeared.

The IJNAF had a selection process to determine ability, dividing trainees between those selected for flight training and those who would become observers, navigators, bombardiers, radio operators, and gunners. There were specialist training schools to teach these skills, with the bombardier/observer course at three of the IJNAF's training bases lasting from 12 to 14 months and including 300 hours of flying time, with half the time devoted to practice bombing with live bombs.

Aichi built 24 H9As in 1940–42 to serve as advanced trainers for pilots destined to fly the H8K. Behind this example is one of 20 Yokosuka H5Y1s constructed in 1938–41, which were also relegated to training duties after they were found to be too underpowered for frontline use. (Tony Holmes Collection)

1. Control column	13. Intake pressure control lever	23. Vertical pitch gauge	33. Vacuum gauge
2. Aileron control wheel	14. Engine ignition controls	24. Flightpath indicator	34. Exhaust temperature gauges
3. Vertical pitch gauge	15. Mixture controls	25. Airspeed indicator	35. Aileron trim tab control handle
4. Airspeed indicator	16. Propeller pitch controls	26. Turn indicator	
5. Turn indicator	17. Two-speed supercharger selector	27. Climb indicator	36. Flap control lever
6. Compass	18. Throttle levers	28. Compass	37. Rudder trim tab control handle
7. Climb indicator	19. Engine ignition switches	29. Artificial horizon	
8. Artificial horizon	20. Boost gauges	30. Mixture gauge	38. Heater air vents
9. Altimeter	21. Type 0 autopilot control panel	31. Supercharger pressure gauges	39. Rudder pedals
10. Flap angle indicator	22. Altimeter	32. Autopilot adjustment switches	40. Co-pilot's seat
11. Tachometer			41. Pilot's seat
12. Landing attitude warning light			

Many H8K pilots came to the large flying boat having trained or served a combat tour on the earlier H6Ks. Others had spent time flying shore or ship-based floatplane reconnaissance aircraft like the Kawanishi Type 94 Reconnaissance Seaplane E7K1 and E7K2, shown here on the deck of the seaplane tender *Mizuho* off Tsingtao, China, in 1939. (NH82456, NHHC)

The standard course for radio operators lasted 12 months, with the first half devoted to learning Morse code and the second half spent practicing sending and receiving messages in an aircraft. Radio operators also received basic instruction in operating machine guns.

Gunnery training took place at Kasumigaura and the IJN's arsenal at Suzuka, southwest of Nagoya. The initial course lasted six months, with the first three months devoted to basic gunnery and operation of the 7.7mm machine gun. The second half of the course included air-to-air firing of flexible machine guns from Mitsubishi Type 90 (K3M3) single-engined crew training aircraft against towed sleeves. After completing the basic course, gunnery trainees undertook several more months of tuition in advanced operational aircraft such as the Mitsubishi Type 96 Attack Bomber (G3M).

During the war a large Rengo Kokutai (combined air group) with bases in Japan and China trained navigators, radio operators, and air gunners. With the IJN's strict system of seniority, it was normal for the highest ranking member of the aircrew to be the aircraft commander, whether he was a pilot or not. Following devastating losses of H6Ks to Allied fighters over the Solomons in late 1942, the IJNAF instituted more intensive gunnery training at unit level and at the basic gunnery schools.

Combat attrition steadily reduced the cadre of pre-war pilots and crews. In order to increase the number of pilots and observers reaching the frontline as attrition replacement, the IJNAF had to streamline its training programs. It delayed the implementation of any major changes until 1943, when the IJNAF expanded its training through the formation of more Rengo Kokutai dedicated to elementary flight training in Central Honshu. Advanced training air groups were also established in Kyushu and Formosa.

Pilots who subsequently completed the accelerated programs from 1943 lacked the skills and experience of their peers, and had less capacity to undertake operations. Some Kokutai began reporting the number of crews on hand that were capable of flying missions at night and those that were qualified only for day missions. One experienced H8K pilot recalled that toward the end of 1943, when his unit was stationed at Jaluit, there were not many crews left who were capable of flying night missions. The quality of IJNAF aircrew continued to decline as the war went on, increasing the burden placed on the surviving experienced crews.

COMBAT

Encounters between US Navy PB4Y-1 Liberators and IJNAF H6Ks and H8Ks were infrequent and mostly random occurrences. The PB4Y squadrons usually had a complement of 12 aircraft to conduct three to four single aircraft search missions a day. Each Liberator covered a sector nine degrees wide, with an outgoing leg, a crossing leg at the end of the sector, and a return leg. Sector length varied, from 500 to 1,000 miles, with 800 miles being the average distance. Most patrols flew at an altitude of around 8,000ft. An 800-mile sector took a little over ten hours to complete, while a 1,000-mile sector could take more than 13 hours and involve a night landing.

Once over enemy-held territory, gun positions were manned at all times, with the crews rotating the duty. Maintaining a sharp lookout was the only way to avoid being attacked, to observe and report the findings of the patrol, and to spot enemy aircraft. Successful attacks depended on early sighting and identification of the enemy, the PB4Y moving into position for an advantageous pass before the enemy aircraft could react. Excellent gunnery then ensured the opponent's destruction.

The three IJNAF flying boat Kokutai appear to have followed a similar pattern when it came to operations, sending out three H8Ks to cover contiguous sectors up to 700 miles from their bases in Japan to the Dutch East Indies. The older H6K transport flying boats and the H8K transports flew regular runs between Japanese bases. Higher IJN commands also regularly called on the flying boat units to assist the dedicated H8K transports by carrying passengers and supplies from Japan to the island bases across the Pacific.

Having entered service before the outbreak of the Pacific War, the H6K was already known to USAAC and US Navy intelligence, who had a reasonable idea of its performance characteristics and armament. This information was available in official manuals on the identification of Japanese aircraft. During the aerial combats fought

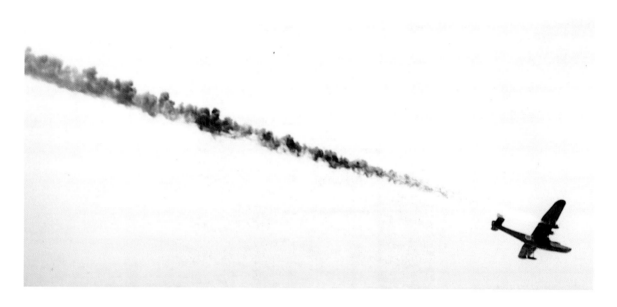

The first PB4Y victory against a Japanese flying boat came on 28 August 1943 when Lt John Alley and his crew from VB-104, flying from Carney Field on Guadalcanal, encountered an H6K transport and shot it down in flames. (80G-81958, RG80, NARA)

at the time of the retaking of Guadalcanal in August 1942, US Navy fighters shot down several H6Ks. These one-sided actions provided additional information on the type's strengths and weaknesses.

In the fall of 1942 Capt Frank McCoy and his team in the Material Section, Directorate of Intelligence, Allied Air Forces Southwest Pacific Area, chose the reporting name "Mavis" for the Type 97. When Lt C. J. Alley and his crew from VB-104 ran into an H6K during a patrol on August 28, 1943, in the first encounter between a US Navy PB4Y-1 and a Japanese flying boat, he knew to avoid the 20mm cannon in the "Mavis'" tail turret.

The US Navy had established VB-104 at NAS Kaneohe Bay, Hawaii, as a PB4Y-1 Liberator squadron in April 1943, manning the unit by splitting off a group of pilots and crews from PBY-equipped VP-71. The new squadron continued flying patrols in PBYs until its crews could pick up new PB4Y-1s in San Diego and fly them back to Hawaii for training. On August 15 VB-104 moved to Carney Field on Guadalcanal to replace VB-101 (the first PB4Y-1 squadron in the Southwest Pacific). Within four days of its arrival, the unit began flying bombing and patrol missions, covering 12 sectors fanning out from northwest to the east of Guadalcanal and the Solomon Islands chain and northeast beyond the island of Nauru.

On August 28, the squadron assigned Lt John Alley and his crew coverage of Sector 2 (east of the Solomons) on a clear and sunny day with excellent visibility. A little after noon, as their PB4Y was flying on the homeward leg of their patrol, the crew sighted a "Mavis" flying 15 miles ahead of the Liberator off the port bow. The H6K was at 8,000ft transiting the route from Truk to Rabaul, while the PB4Y was at 5,000ft. Alley climbed to get into a position below the "Mavis," keeping the belly turret retracted so as to increase his climbing speed.

As the PB4Y neared the H6K, bow turret gunner AMM2c Lyme Lymenstull used the rings on his gunsight to give the other gunners the range to the enemy aircraft. There was no indication that the "Mavis" had seen the approaching PB4Y until, at a range of just 500 yards, the Liberator gunners opened fire. By coincidence, a year

This H8K1 discovered in the lagoon at Butaritari Island after the capture of Makin Atoll in November 1943 provided US Naval Intelligence with the first details on the "Emily's" characteristics and performance. This find came shortly before the first encounter between a PB4Y and a Type 2 Flying Boat on December 1, 1943. (80G-307463, RG80, NARA)

earlier, gunners on a "Mavis" had shot at Lymenstull while he was flying in a PBY, and now he had an opportunity to get revenge. He fired four long bursts from the bow turret, getting hits in the No. 4 engine, then the No. 3 engine, and as the "Mavis" banked to starboard, hitting the Nos. 2 and 1 engines as well.

The top turret and the port waist gun also fired, and in just seven seconds all four of the flying boat's engines were on fire, with flames and a long stream of smoke pouring aft. The "Mavis" spiraled down to crash into the sea below. There was no return fire. This was a transport version of the aircraft, most likely an H6K4-L serving with the 11th Koku Sentai. It would be four months before the next encounter between a PB4Y and a Japanese flying boat.

Until the end of 1943, the H8K was something of an enigma. Allied intelligence knew that the Japanese had developed a new four-engined flying boat, and the aircraft was assigned the reporting name "Emily." However, it was not known if this was a development of the H6K or a completely new type. A photograph of a large flying boat at Makin Atoll taken in July 1943 and a blurry air-to-air image captured the following month gave a crude outline of the fuselage, the single vertical, tail and what the photo interpreters thought was a gull wing.

US Navy Grumman F6F-3 Hellcats claimed two of these aircraft shot down in September and one in November, providing more details on the H8K's armament of bow, dorsal and tail turrets, and waist gun positions. A derelict "Emily" found in Makin Atoll after its capture in late November gave US Naval Intelligence an opportunity to conduct a detailed examination of the aircraft, which in turn provided more accurate information on the H8K's configuration and performance, although less on armament because this had probably been removed by the Japanese prior to the flying boat being abandoned. It is unlikely that the first PB4Y crew to encounter an "Emily" had this up-to-date intelligence.

Lt William J. Graham and his crew from VB-108 (another of the early PB4Y squadrons in the Pacific) had taken off from Nukufetau airfield on Mokolatu Island, in the Ellice Islands group southeast of Tarawa, three hours before midnight on

December 1, 1943 on a long patrol mission of 950 miles to the northwest of his base. While flying at 2,000ft at the base of clouds, and nearing the end of the sector 350 miles west of Tarawa, Graham's tail gunner sighted an aircraft well behind the PB4Y. The crew lost sight of the contact in the clouds, but on climbing to 5,500ft, above the cloud tops, it regained contact and set off in a pursuit that lasted 30 minutes. The Japanese flying boat, identified as an "Emily," continued on its course and altitude, and as recorded in the Aircraft Action Report:

> It seemed as if her watchers were not alert for she did not open fire until some 45 seconds after the PB4Y closed to within 500 yards and opened up with both turrets, top and bow, from dead astern and 200ft below.

The "Emily" pilot immediately dove his aircraft and straightened out below the PB4Y, the 20mm cannon in the tail turret opening up on the Liberator when it was slightly above and to starboard. The PB4Y's gunners had set the "Emily's" No. 4 engine on fire, which slewed the flying boat to starboard. With the Japanese aircraft only 200ft ahead of the Liberator, the PB4Y gunners knocked out the tail and top turrets, but the "Emily's" waist 20mm position then opened fire. The PB4Y was hit in the cockpit, wounding Graham in the feet and his co-pilot, Ens Ralph Cook, in the left arm and right hand, destroying the radio compass and the artificial horizon. Return fire from the "Emily" also shot two feet off the starboard aileron and put holes in the port flap and port rudder.

After the exchange of fire, the crew could see fuel pouring out of the "Emily's" starboard wing, but they were surprised that the Japanese aircraft did not explode as so many others had done before it. The flying boat dived away into the clouds with its No. 4 engine and starboard wing on fire and the No. 2 engine smoking, but the PB4Y crew did not see the Japanese aircraft crash. Cook took over from Graham and brought the PB4Y back to land at the airfield on Nanumea, an atoll northwest of Nukufetau, after 14.5 hours in the air. Four days later, another PB4Y from VB-108 destroyed an H8K on the water at Emidj Island, in the Jaluit Atoll, with two 325lb depth charges.

There was another hiatus of four months between the encounters. As the Pacific War advanced progressively westward, so too did the PB4Y squadrons. At the end of March 1944, VB-106 moved from Munda, in the Solomon Islands, operating as part of Fleet Air Wing 1, to Nadzab, on the northern coast of New Guinea, joining Fleet Air Wing 17. The squadron remained at Nadzab for only two weeks before heading to Momote airfield on

VB-106 PB4Y crews are briefed before heading out on patrol. The Liberator and, later, Privateer squadrons mounted three to four patrols a day, covering adjacent sectors, sometimes as far out as 1,000 miles from base on missions that lasted 12+ hours. (208AA, Folder 59, RG208, NARA)

the island of Los Negros, in the Admiralty Islands. From Momote the squadron flew five sector patrols daily, sending PB4Ys out 800 miles on normal patrols, and 1,000 miles in connection with activities of the Pacific Fleet in the area. On one of these patrols, on April 17, 1944, Lt Everett Mitchell and his crew came upon an H6K about 100 miles north of the west coast of New Guinea.

Searching with binoculars from his seat in the cockpit, Mitchell was the first to spot the "Mavis" flying 20 miles from the PB4Y. The latter was heading west, while the H6K was flying to the northeast at 6,000ft at an estimated speed of 173mph. Mitchell was flying at the same speed, but at an altitude of 8,000ft. He immediately turned the PB4Y and set off in pursuit. When he had closed to within five miles of the "Mavis," the crew of the flying boat spotted the PB4Y approaching and dived down to the sea. While the waist and tail gunners engaged the PB4Y when it came within range, the pilot banked the "Mavis" to starboard to throw off the Liberator.

In response, Mitchell applied full power and drew abreast of his opponent at the "nine o'clock" position some 500ft above the flying boat. The PB4Y gunners opened fire at a range of 300 yards as Mitchell closed to 200ft above the "Mavis," and they continued firing until the Liberator had passed beyond their target, setting the No. 3 engine on fire. On the second run Mitchell brought the PB4Y in on the starboard side of the "Mavis," and from "three o'clock high" the gunners again opened fire, seeing smoke pouring out of the center section of the wing. The PB4Y came in for a third run, once again on the port side of the "Mavis" at its "nine o'clock" position. This time the belly turret gunner shot off the flying boat's entire tail section, and seconds later there was an explosion in the wing center section when the unprotected fuel tanks were hit. The H6K crashed into the sea below in flames, the engagement having lasted just four minutes.

As the Aircraft Action Report noted, the "Mavis" was "helpless in the face of the superior firepower and the aggressive attack of the PB4Y." It was H6K4-L J-BGOH of Dai Nippon Airways, undertaking a flight to Palau for the IJN, that had had the

On February 10, 1944, Lt Everett Mitchell ground-looped this VB-106 PB4Y-1 at the airfield on Munda when the left tire blew out, collapsing the left landing gear. Two months later, Mitchell and his crew would have an extraordinary run of luck, downing a "Mavis" on April 17 and an "Emily" one week later. They duly became the only PB4Y crew to shoot down two Japanese flying boats during the war. (NH 74788, NHHC)

misfortune of running into the PB4Y. This was a pattern that would continue in the encounters between the PB4Ys and the IJNAF flying boats, with the Liberators conducting aggressive attacks using multiple guns. Remarkably, exactly one week later (April 24), Mitchell and his crew engaged, and destroyed, an "Emily" to become the only PB4Y crew to down two IJNAF flying boats.

Three more encounters with flying boats would occur through to July 1944, with all of these combats resulting in victories for the PB4Ys. The clashes all took place in the Central Pacific, where the invasion of the Marshall Islands and capture of Kwajalein and Eniwetok had followed the successful occupation of the Gilbert Islands. Kwajalein and then Eniwetok became bases for US Navy patrol squadrons, with VB-108 and VB-109 flying from the latter island on 900-mile patrols toward the Caroline Islands.

Some of the early PB4Y-1s had a Convair 250CH-3 gun turret in the nose instead of the ERCO 250SH-3 ball turret, as seen here on this PB4Y-1 from one of the patrol squadrons based on Kwajalein in March 1944. (80G-407715, RG80, NARA)

On May 7 Lt John Keeling and his crew from VB-109 were on just such a mission to the northern Carolines when the radio operator manning the port waist gun reported an aircraft at 5,000ft some 15 miles ahead above a bank of clouds. The PB4Y, flying at 3,500ft north of the islands, was in turn sighted, and the enemy pilot immediately reversed course. Keeling set off in pursuit and began to climb, quickly closing on what the crew had by now identified was an H6K. To gain speed, Keeling jettisoned the two depth charges he was carrying. The "Mavis" reached the cloud bank before Keeling's gunners came within range. The two aircraft then pursued each other in and out of the clouds for the next 20 minutes, with the "Mavis" turning frequently to seek cover.

Keeling followed the "Mavis" in its turns, and when the Japanese aircraft emerged into clearer skies on the starboard side of the PB4Y, the bow turret gunner started firing. The PB4Y was then flying at 1,500ft, with the "Mavis" above it. The latter made a turn to port, enabling the bow and top turret gunners in the PB4Y to rake the Nos. 3 and 4 engines and the starboard wing. As the Liberator flew past, the starboard waist gunner and then the tail turret got in more bursts. The "Mavis" began firing back at the PB4Y from the tail turret, fuselage, and waist gun positions, but only a single round hit the Liberator, in the bow turret.

Passing through cloud once again, Keeling came out below and 500 yards behind the "Mavis." The bow turret gunner duly disabled the flying boat's tail turret, and as Keeling closed to within 100ft of his quarry, the bow and top turret gunners set fire to one of the fuel tanks within the starboard wing. Flames from the burning wing quickly damaged the "Mavis'" starboard rudder and horizontal stabilizer, and as the flying boat entered a terminal dive toward the sea, the PB4Y gunners continued firing. Shortly thereafter the starboard wing collapsed, causing the H6K to crash into the water and explode.

In May 1944 Gen MacArthur had decided to capture Wakde Island off the northern coast of western New Guinea in order to build an airfield on it that could support operations in the Mariana and Palau Islands group, and the continued movement west toward the Philippines, planned for later in the year. Soon after the capture of Wakde at the end of May, VB-115 moved seven PB4Y aircraft to the new airfield to begin daily patrols west to Halmahera Island and two sectors covering 800 miles toward the approaches to the Philippines. During the month of June these patrols destroyed ten Japanese aircraft, including a single H8K on June 4, 1944.

On that date Lt Hamilton Dawes and his crew sortied from Wakde on one of the long patrol sectors toward the Philippines, flying at 8,000ft through scattered cloud on a course to the northwest. Late in the morning the crew saw a Mitsubishi G4M "Betty" bomber flying below them, only to then lose sight of it in the clouds. At a little after 1300 hrs local time, the crew spotted an "Emily" flying 1,000ft directly above the PB4Y on a westerly course. The PB4Y began to climb, and as it did so, the H8K entered a straight glide, with the Liberator in pursuit.

Dawes climbed to a position 2,000ft above the "Emily" and followed it as, to his surprise, the flying boat stuck to a straight course rather than seeking cover in the clouds. When the "Emily" leveled off at lower altitude, the PB4Y, flying at 230mph, quickly caught up and the gunners opened fire from the bow, top, and belly turrets – they targeted the engines, wing roots, and dorsal turret. One engine immediately fell off under concentrated fire, while the remaining three soon began smoking. The dorsal turret gunner in the "Emily" got off four bursts that failed to hit the PB4Y before return fire knocked it out.

With all engines in flames and smoking, the "Emily" pilot made an excellent water landing. The flying boat sank slowly, and the PB4Y crew saw seven or eight survivors getting into a life raft. As the Liberator left the area, the crew spotted another "Betty" approaching to circle the wreckage of the H8K. Short on fuel, the PB4Y headed back to Wakde Island. The only damage it had suffered in the combat were a few 7.7mm machine gun hits in the tail. In Dawes' opinion, the "Emily" pilot had had many opportunities to escape should he have chosen to find cloud cover, but he had failed to do so. The lack of return fire made the crew wonder if the flying boat was in fact unarmed.

A little over two weeks later, on June 19, a crew from VB-101 shot down another "Emily" during a long patrol from Los Negros.

On May 7, 1944, VB-109's Lt John Keeling and his crew downed a "Mavis" while on patrol near the Caroline Islands. Keeling's gunners quickly set fire to the flying boat's highly vulnerable fuel tanks, and flames streaming back damaged the starboard horizontal stabilizer and rudder. The lack of gun blisters and dorsal and nose gun positions identifies this as an unarmed H6K4-L transport. (80G-227384, RG80, NARA)

ENGAGING THE ENEMY

During World War II, ERCO built gun turrets for the US Navy, beginning with the ERCO 250SH installed in the PB4Y-1. The ERCO turret incorporated two pre-war developments in US Navy aviation ordnance, the 0.50-cal Browning M2 machine gun and the reflector gunsight. As military aircraft acquired armor protection and self-sealing fuel tanks, the US Navy realized the 0.30-cal machine gun was no longer adequate against modern aircraft. The US Navy duly switched to the 0.50-cal machine gun as its principal weapon for fighters and, when placed in powered turrets and free gun positions, its patrol aircraft too.

The US Navy also recognized that its pre-war "ring and post" gunsights gave a limited estimation of the necessary deflection needed to hit a fast-moving target, while its telescopic sights limited freedom of eye movement. The reflector gunsight offered more freedom of vision, with

greater accuracy in calculating deflection. For its free guns and gun turrets, the US Navy developed the Illuminated Sight Mark 9 (seen here) from a British design it had acquired just before the start of the Pacific War.

The bow turret gunner was often the first to open fire when a PB4Y attacked a Japanese aircraft. PPCs would try to maneuver their Liberators and Privateers so that they approached their targets from the rear, above or below, thus allowing as many turret guns to be brought to bear on the enemy aircraft as possible. The bow turret gunners would commence firing at a range of about 500 yards, walking their fire up to the escaping Japanese aircraft when it was flying low over the water. The PB4Y gunners soon learned to knock out the "Emily's" dorsal and tail turrets, allowing their aircraft to close with the flying boat so that they could then concentrate their fire on the H8K's unprotected engines.

A PB4Y-1 from VB-102 lands on the airfield at Tinian in late 1944. This unit shared the base with fellow Liberator squadrons VB-116 and VB-117. During October of that year the US Navy re-designated all multi-engined VB units as VPB squadrons. (San Diego Air and Space Museum)

The squadron had returned to combat after reforming in the United States, replacing VB-106 on Los Negros and sending out daily patrols over four search sectors to the northwest. Initially, the sectors ranged out 800 to 1,000 miles, but between June 15–23, coinciding with Operation *Forager* (the invasion of Saipan), the squadron extended the sectors to 1,100 miles.

On one of these extended patrols on June 19, while flying at 8,000ft in the late morning under scattered clouds, Lt(jg) George Winter and his crew saw an H8K flying below them at 2,000ft on the same general course. This may have been an aircraft from the 851st Kokutai based at Davao, on the island of Mindanao, on a flight to Yap or Palau. Winter flew the PB4Y back into the clouds until all the gunners were ready, then dove down on the "Emily," reaching a speed of 334mph.

As the PB4Y came in on the H8K from "four o'clock," the bow gunner opened fire at 1,000ft behind the flying boat, walking his rounds up the fuselage to the cockpit area. The "Emily" returned fire from its dorsal turret, which the PB4Y crew believed to be light 7.7mm machine gun rounds, until the PB4Y bow gunner shot out the turret. Winter made an "S" turn to keep from overshooting, and as he did so, the bow gunner fired at the inboard engines, setting both on fire. As the "Emily" turned away to starboard, the PB4Y passed overhead, giving the starboard waist gunner and his counterpart in the tail turret a chance to fire, setting the H8K's No. 4 engine alight. Moments later the "Emily" went into a spin, hit the water, and exploded.

Commenting on the Aircraft Action Report, VB-101's commanding officer praised Winter's ability to maneuver his heavily loaded PB4Y in the attack and the "extremely accurate" fire from all the PB4Y's gun positions. In contrast, he said "the ineffective return fire and lack of defense action by the Emily are surprising."

VB-115 had its second encounter with an H8K on July 2, 1944 when Lt Stoughton Atwood and his crew were returning to Wakde Island, having reached the end of their 800-mile patrol sector. While flying at 10,000ft through cumulus clouds, co-pilot Ens R. S. Snoddy saw an "Emily" skirting around a cloud five miles away at 9,500ft. Atwood went to military power and began a climbing turn to approach the H8K from its port quarter. The PB4Y overran the flying boat on this first pass, but gunners manning the bow and top turrets, starboard waist and tail turret all got in good bursts of fire. These knocked out the "Emily's" tail and dorsal turrets and raked the fuselage.

Following this initial pass, the crew could see flame and smoke emitting from the damaged fuselage just above the hull step, and the port engines were also alight. As the H8K descended in a straight glide, Atwood brought the PB4Y back around for another pass. Cutting his throttles, he kept his Liberator on the "Emily's" quarter, giving his gunners excellent position at close range. Now on fire, the flying boat pulled up into a stall, recovered, and then went up into a stall again, this time falling off in a terminal dive down toward the sea, its wings and tail coming off just prior to the H8K exploding upon hitting the water.

Photographs taken of the flying boat during the combat showed its tail number as "51-085," indicating an aircraft from the 851st Kokutai. Atwood noted in his Aircraft Action Report that the "Emily" appeared to have been taken completely by surprise, with the waist gun hatches remaining closed until after the PB4Y's fire had crippled the flying boat's armament during its first pass. A pattern was now emerging in the IJNAF flying boat crews' responses to attack. Once again, as in the earlier combat on June 4, return fire directed at the attacking PB4Y and the minimal evasive maneuvers made by the pilot were ineffective.

There was another long gap of four months between encounters. By October 1944, the PB4Y patrol squadrons had moved westward from Eniwetok to Tinian and come back under Fleet Air Wing 1 control. Three units were now based on Tinian, having been re-designated VPB squadrons to distinguish the US Navy's land-based patrol bombers from its carrier-based dive-bombers, who also used the VB designation. At Tinian, VPB-102 served with sister squadrons VPB-116 and VPB-117. From their base, the three PB4Y units covered 12 patrol sectors from the southwest toward the Philippines, west to the Ryukyu Islands and north along the Nampo Shoto Islands, which included Iwo Jima. The PB4Y-1s ranged out 1,000 miles, carrying a full load of fuel to extend their range if a suitable contact appeared on the AN/APS-15 ASV search radar that many of the aircraft now carried.

On October 31, Lt Herbert Box and his crew from VPB-117 had flown 980 miles out from Tinian on their sector patrol, completed the cross leg and were flying southeast on a course for base when the starboard waist gunner saw an aircraft at "three o'clock" to the PB4Y some 35 miles away on a course to the northwest. The contact resembled a US Navy PBM flying boat, but a check of the charts confirmed that the target was well outside the Mariner patrol

In September 1944, VB-117 joined VB-102 and VB-116 on Tinian. On October 31, VB-117's Lt Herbert Box and his crew shot down an "Emily" they had encountered on the final leg of their patrol. Box's gunners set the flying boat's Nos. 2 and 3 engines on fire, as seen in this dramatic photograph taken from the PBY4-1. (80G-190205, RG80, NARA)

sectors, so it was likely to be a Japanese flying boat. Box reversed course, and after viewing the aircraft with his binoculars, determined that it was indeed an "Emily." Photographs taken of the flying boat during the ensuing combat identified the aircraft as "801-77" from the 801st Kokutai.

Box decided to engage the "Emily," and to save fuel for the chase he jettisoned the PB4Y-1's three 250lb bombs. The H8K remained on course, only increasing its speed as the Liberator began to close in a pursuit that lasted 35 minutes. The PB4Y reached a speed of 200mph – less than the maximum speed of the "Emily" – yet it began to close on the Japanese aircraft. When he was 15 miles away, Box increased his speed to 224mph, and coming in from a higher altitude, nosed down to pick up more speed as he approached from the "five o'clock" position. The "Emily" did not attempt any evasive action, apart from dropping down to 500ft above the ocean.

When the PB4Y was 500 yards away from the "Emily," the bow gunner opened fire, concentrating on the No. 3 engine and then switching to the No. 2 engine. With the latter soon on fire, the pilot of the "Emily" banked the aircraft to port, with the PB4Y following, continuing the attack from the "five o'clock" position and above. As Box steepened his dive, the top turret gunner and the port waist gunner opened fire on the "Emily" at a range of 300 yards, setting the flying boat's No. 3 engine on fire.

The "Emily" turned to starboard to evade the diving PB4Y, but the speed of the pursuing Liberator meant that Box could not turn inside the aircraft, forcing him to pass over the top of the H8K. This, however, gave his starboard waist gunner an opportunity to open fire, getting more hits on the Nos. 2 and 3 engines. As the PB4Y

With its engines on fire, the "Emily" pilot lost control and the aircraft slammed into the ocean, tearing itself apart. (80G-275596, RG80, NARA)

pulled ahead of the "Emily," the Japanese aircraft began to lose speed and descend toward the ocean, with the Nos. 2 and 3 engines on fire. As the PB4Y's tail gunner targeted the cockpit area, the "Emily" crashed into the water.

In another example of ineffective gunnery, when the PB4Y had reached a position 400 yards behind the flying boat in its initial attack, the tail and dorsal turret gunners opened fire with their 20mm cannon. The Liberator crew estimated as many as 200 rounds were fired by the IJNAF gunners, but only one hit the PB4Y in the port wingtip. The remaining rounds passed underneath or behind the patrol bomber.

The next day (November 1), it was VPB-117's sister squadron VPB-116 that encountered an H8K in one of the most remarkable engagements between a US Navy patrol bomber and an IJNAF flying boat. Early that morning, VPB-116 had received word that the submarine USS *Salmon* (SS-182) had been badly damaged in combat with IJN anti-submarine patrol vessels and was unable to submerge. *Salmon* called on three nearby submarines, USS *Silversides* (SS-236), USS *Trigger* (SS-237), and USS *Sterlet* (SS-392), to escort it back to Saipan on the surface. As *Salmon* was only 450 miles from Kyushu and Japanese bases in the Ryukyus, there was a significant risk of air attack. It was assumed that the "Emily" VPB-117 shot down the day before was searching for the American submarine.

Air cover would be necessary to get *Salmon* safely to Saipan, so early in the morning of the 1st VPB-116 sortied Lt Guy Thompson and his crew to fly cover over the submarines and shoot down any IJNAF aircraft attempting to attack the US Navy vessels. Thompson's PB4Y-1 was fitted with an AN/APS-15 ASV search radar in place of its belly turret and RCM instruments in the form of a receiver (possibly an AN/APR-5 radar intercept receiver subsequently fitted as standard to the PB4Y-2 Privateer) that could pick up radar emissions.

In Thompson's crew, Aviation Chief Radio Technician (ACRT) W. T. Kane manned the RCM equipment and Aviation Chief Radioman (ACRM) E. F. Bryant operated the search radar. Someone, possibly ACRT Kane, realized that if there were IJNAF aircraft searching for the American submarines, it was possible that they would be using Japanese ASV search radar, and that the radar emissions from these aircraft could be used to locate them in the air.

At 1100 hrs, when the PB4Y was more than four hours into its patrol and on the way to the estimated location of the submarines, ACRT Kane, who was monitoring his RCM instruments, intercepted an enemy radar transmission that he estimated was between 75 to 90 miles away from his aircraft. Analyzing the radar pulses, Kane noticed that they had only two amplitudes, indicating that they came from a stationary rather than a rotating antenna, and that the signal did not correspond with Japanese submarine radar, strongly suggesting that the emissions were coming from an IJNAF aircraft.

Shortly after intercepting the first emission, Kane located a second signal. Due to the limitations of his equipment, he could not give Thompson an accurate bearing on the Japanese aircraft. As the radar pulses became stronger, Kane estimated that one aircraft was 30 miles from the PB4Y and the second slightly further away.

Immediately after Kane had first picked up the enemy radar emissions, ACRM Bryant lowered the ASV search radar and began looking for the enemy aircraft. Thirty minutes after the initial intercept of the enemy radar pulses, Bryant picked up a "bogey" on his radar at "1.30 o'clock low" and nine-and-a-half miles distant from the PB4Y. At the same moment that Bryant reported the contact, a crewman called in a visual sighting of an "Emily" – the PB4Y crew noted in their Aircraft Action Report that the flying boat did indeed have a radar antenna attached.

Thompson let the "Emily" pass to starboard before initiating a 180-degree turn to come in behind the flying boat, which was ten miles ahead of the PB4Y. Thompson, however, had an altitude advantage as he was flying around 5,000ft above the H8K, and he used this to pick up speed, nosing over into a glide and closing the gap to eight miles. At this point the "Emily" sighted the approaching PB4Y and increased its speed from 167mph to 219mph. For a brief time the flying boat increased the separation, but Thompson put on more power and went into a steeper dive, building his speed up to 299mph and closing to a point 2,000ft behind and 500ft above the "Emily."

It was then that the bow turret gunner opened fire, aiming at the dorsal turret,

The day after Lt Box's victory on October 31, 1944, it was VPB-116's turn to shoot down an "Emily" when Lt Guy Thompson and his crew used their radar countermeasures equipment and ASV search radar to locate the H8K that was searching for a damaged US Navy submarine. Here, the "Emily" banks to port after Thompson's bow turret gunner has come within range to open fire. (80G-190203, RG80, NARA)

knocking it out, and starting a fire in the No. 1 engine. The "Emily" pilot banked steeply to the left, almost standing the aircraft on its wingtip according to the PB4Y crew. Thompson followed the turn and again overtook the H8K from the starboard side. The bow, top turret, and port waist guns immediately opened fire, hitting the engines and the wings. The experienced "Emily" pilot turned into the PB4Y so as to get the flying boat's bow turret into position to fire on the Liberator, but Thompson slid his aircraft over the H8K, giving the bow turret, starboard waist, and tail turret gunners a chance to fire. He then racked his PB4Y around in a violent 180-degree turn to get back into position to attack the "Emily," which was now down to just 50ft off the water, from behind.

To increase speed, the H8K jettisoned its depth charges from beneath the wings in the hope that the resulting explosions might damage the oncoming PB4Y, but Thompson quickly pulled up to 500ft, passing over the geysers of water that erupted when the ordnance exploded. Thompson again dropped down on the "Emily's" starboard side, only to find that his bow and top turret guns had jammed. As he pulled ahead, however, the port waist and tail turret gunners got in more strikes on the now-slowing "Emily," which turned to port to evade the attack.

Thompson jettisoned his own depth charges at this point, before coming in again above and slightly behind the flying boat, pushing the PB4Y's nose down to give the

The PB4Y squadrons shot down three Japanese flying boats during December 1944, with VPB-101 and VPB-104 each claiming a "Mavis." On the 28th, the gunners of Lt Edward Hagen's VPB-104 crew set the center wing tanks of Dai Nippon Koku H6K4-L transport J-BGOA on fire. The subsequent explosion tore off the flying boat's starboard wing. (80G-296951, RG80, NARA)

bow turret gunner, with his guns now cleared, a chance to rake the "Emily" from point-blank range – the resulting fire set the H8K's Nos. 3 and 4 engine alight. Its starboard wing float hit the water moments later, tearing off the starboard wing and sending the flying boat cartwheeling into the water to explode.

After returning to Tinian and going over the action and the relative positions of the Japanese aircraft and the American submarines, the squadron determined that the H8K had come close to intercepting *Salmon* and its three escorts, having been just 40 miles away. Using search radar and a square search pattern, the "Emily" would have found the American submarines if the Liberator had not intercepted it.

During the action the PB4Y had received negligible damage from the "Emily's" return fire, the aircraft having suffered just two machine gun hits near the port and starboard waist hatches. While the return fire was ineffective, Thompson stated in the Aircraft Action Report that he was impressed with the evasive maneuvers employed by his opponent. Violent turns had been accomplished with "evident ease," although ultimately to no avail. The report also noted that "it is believed that this is the first reported instance of a plane being picked up by RCM gear and identified positively as enemy on the basis of a difference in frequency." It also appears to have been the first, and possibly only, time during the war that a US Navy aircraft used RCM instrumentation in combination with airborne search radar to locate an enemy aircraft.

In the final months of the year the PB4Y squadrons shot down two H6Ks and a single H8K. For the Liberator crews, by this late stage of the Pacific War combats with

the "Mavis" were straightforward. It was simply a matter of getting the PB4Y into a position where the gunners could shoot out the engines and set the wing fuel tanks on fire. Destruction of the flying boat inevitably followed.

On November 22, Lt Albert Bellsey and his crew from VPB-101, now based on Morotai, west of New Guinea, found a "Mavis" flying near the Celebes, east of Borneo. During the PB4Y's first pass, the bow and belly turret gunners set the "Mavis'" No. 2 engine on fire, and in the second pass all four engines burst into flames, blowing off the starboard wing.

After the capture of Leyte, the US Navy moved several PB4Y squadrons and detachments to the airfield at Tacloban for patrolling the South China Sea west of the Philippines as far as the coast of French Indochina. On December 28, Lt(jg) Edward Hagen and his crew from VPB-104 took off from Tacloban on just such a patrol – these missions saw Liberators cover more than 1,000 miles. Flying at 7,500ft, they sighted a "Mavis" approaching them at 10,000ft. Again, this was a Dai Nippon Koku H6K4-L transport, specifically aircraft J-BGOA flying the route from Saigon, in French Indochina, to southern Formosa.

Hagen pulled his aircraft around in a turn to starboard and began climbing after the "Mavis," increasing power. Reaching 8,500ft, the PB4Y was underneath and slightly behind the H6K when Hagen gave the command to open fire. The bow and top turret gunners fired, hitting the No. 3 engine, which began smoking. The bow turret's machine guns then jammed, but the top turret continued firing in short,

The "Emily" pilot attempted to crash into Lt Squires' PB4Y-1 as he passed over the Japanese flying boat but failed, and moments later the H8K from the 801st Kokutai exploded when it crashed into the South China Sea. (80G-311106, RG80, NARA)

continuous bursts. The "Mavis" nosed over and headed toward a large cloud, making gentle turns to throw off the PB4Y's aim, but without success. Having cleared the jam, the bow turret gunner opened fire again, and hits from both turrets caused an explosion in the starboard wing, tearing it off the flying boat. The H6K spun down and crashed into the sea.

The last combat of the year with a Japanese flying boat took place two days later, on December 30, when a PB4Y crew from VPB-117 sighted an H8K while patrolling off Formosa. That morning, Lt Graham Squires and his crew were over the South China Sea to the southwest of the southern tip of Formosa, flying on a westerly course at 6,000ft between two layers of cloud. The PB4Y was just below the upper cloud layer when the top turret gunner called out an "Emily" flying at the aircraft's "three o'clock" position around 18 miles away to the southeast.

Squires quickly climbed into the clouds to avoid being spotted by the flying boat. Making effective use of the cloud layer, Squires had closed the range to just six miles when the "Emily" crew spotted the approaching PB4Y. The flying boat immediately turned and headed back in the direction of Formosa, with Squires in pursuit, diving into the lower cloud layer to escape. The radar operator on board the PB4Y quickly found the "Emily" on his AN/APS-15 radar scope and directed Squires toward the enemy aircraft, which had descended below the lower cloud layer and dived down toward the ocean, pulling out at 150ft. Squires closed the range and leveled off above the H8K at 200ft.

Although the PB4Y was still out of 0.50-cal range, the "Emily's" dorsal and tail 20mm turret gunners opened fire but scored no hits on the Liberator. Coming in quickly, the PB4Y's bow turret gunner shot out the dorsal turret, then set the No. 3 engine on fire. The top turret gunner also hit the "Emily" moments later. Squires

The improved PB4Y-2 began replacing the PB4Y-1 in the US Navy's land-based patrol units from late 1944, with VPB-118 being the first Privateer squadron to reach the Pacific in early 1945. From their base on Tinian, Lt Norman Keiser and his crew claimed an "Emily" shot down on March 11, 1945 for VPB-118's first aerial victory. (80G-407352, RG80, NARA)

reduced power to avoid overshooting the flying boat, but as he was about to cross over the H8K, its pilot pulled his aircraft up sharply in an attempt to crash into the PB4Y. Squires slammed the throttles forward and pulled the Liberator up and over the "Emily," missing the Japanese aircraft by just 25ft. The mortally wounded H8K, from the 801st Kokutai, fell away to starboard and crashed into the ocean.

There was again a hiatus in clashes between PB4Ys and IJNAF flying boats following the action on December 30. This ended on March 11, 1945, when, in the bizarre randomness of aerial combat over the vast Pacific Ocean, two PB4Y squadrons each shot down an H8K within six days of each other. The two combats took place hundreds of miles apart and under different circumstances. The March 11 action resulted in the first aerial victory for VPB-118 – the first PB4Y-2 Privateer unit to enter combat in the Pacific. The second, six days later, relied on code-breaking and signals intelligence – areas where the US Navy again enjoyed a significant technological advantage over the IJNAF.

VPB-118 had been established in July 1944 as a Patrol Bombing Squadron, initially flying PB4Y-1s until it transitioned to larger PB4Y-2s the following month. The unit arrived on Tinian on January 10, 1945 to begin a tour with Fleet Air Wing 1. VPB-118 soon started flying long patrols of 600 to 1,000 miles to the west and north of Tinian.

On March 11 Lt Norman Keiser and his crew were at the northern end of their patrol sector, just east of the Ryukyu Island chain, flying at 2,000ft. The crew sighted two H8Ks at 7,000ft flying with seven twin-engined aircraft, identified by Keiser's crew as Kawasaki Type 2 Two-seat Fighters (Ki-45 "Nicks"). They assumed the "Emilys" were escorting the "Nicks" on a ferry mission, but it is possible that the flying boats and the twin-engined aircraft were in fact part of an intended Kamikaze mission targeting the US Navy anchorage at Ulithi Atoll.

The IJNAF had dispatched 24 Yokosuka P1Y1 Ginga bombers (Allied reporting name "Frances") from the Azusa Special Attack Unit, with H8Ks from the 801st Kokutai as escorts. Five to six of the P1Y1 bombers, which bore a passing resemblance to Ki-45s, had to return to base with engine problems, and it may have been this somewhat depleted group that Keiser and his crew encountered. Three of the aircraft they had identified as "Nicks" flew out to take a look at the PB4Y-2 after the crew noticed that Japanese radar had picked up the Privateer, but they made no attempt at an interception.

Shortly thereafter, the crew spotted another "Emily," possibly unrelated to the mission to Ulithi, flying at 5,000ft on a reciprocal course at "three o'clock" to the PB4Y-2. Keiser increased power on his aircraft and began a climbing turn to starboard to intercept the "Emily." He caught up with the flying boat, approaching from the "five o'clock" position before nosing over to come in slightly below the "Emily." With the H8K now at "11 o'clock," the bow turret gunner opened fire, hitting the "Emily's" vertical stabilizer.

Keiser then skidded his aircraft to port to put the PB4Y-2 between the sun and the H8K so as to make it harder for the enemy gunners to acquire the Privateer. In response, the "Emily" nosed over into a dive and picked up speed, turning to starboard. As the flying boat accelerated and reached a point 800 yards ahead of the PB4Y-2, the latter's bow, forward, and aft top turrets, as well as the starboard ERCO waist turret, opened fire until the PB4Y-2 was just 200 yards away. Rounds knocked out the "Emily's" port waist 20mm cannon, which had been steadily firing on the PB4Y-2. Fire broke out in the H8K's port wing, and the No. 2 engine fell off the flying boat as it dived out of control and hit the water – a large column of black smoke rose 5,000ft in the air from the spot where the "Emily" crashed. On their return to Tinian, Keiser and his men were bought drinks by VBP-118's remaining crews as a reward for scoring the squadron's first aerial victory.

Six days later (March 17), it was the turn of the veteran VPB-104, now flying from Clark Field on Luzon in the Philippines, to see aerial action. For Lt Paul Stevens and his crew, the day began like any other with a mission briefing. His crew and three others from VPB-104 were to carry out patrols over the South China Sea, with Stevens assigned to a sector between Formosa and the China Coast. The primary mission assigned to the four crews was, however, out of the ordinary.

They were to locate and shoot down an "Emily" that US Naval Intelligence, through radio intercepts, believed to be carrying Vice-Admiral Seigo Yamagata, Commander-in-Chief of the Fourth Southern Expeditionary Fleet in the Dutch East Indies, who was flying back to Tokyo to assume the post of Vice Minister of the Ministry of the Navy as a full admiral. The IJNAF had sent an H8K2-L to transport Yamagata and several staff officers back to Japan, the flying boat departing from Singapore and then heading northeast along the coast of China.

For Stevens and his crew this proved to be an eventful patrol. Upon reaching the east coast of China, Stevens found a 2,000-ton enemy freighter which he attacked and left sinking in flames. Next, the crew sighted two Aichi E13A "Jake" floatplanes flying in formation. The lead aircraft broke off to seek sanctuary over a nearby IJN destroyer, but Stevens maneuvered his PB4Y-1 alongside the second "Jake," and the bow, top and tail turret gunners and the starboard waist gunner shot the IJNAF floatplane down in flames. Stevens then set course for a special orbiting point off the China coast where intelligence believed he would have a chance to intercept the "Emily" transport.

Late in the afternoon, while flying at 2,000ft, the crew saw an H8K approaching them at 3,000ft on a reciprocal course some five miles away. Stevens made a climbing turn and closed the range, his bow and top turret gunners opening fire. Spotting the PB4Y heading for him, the "Emily" pilot increased power but took no evasive action. After the PB4Y began firing, the flying boat went into a gentle glide at full power, reaching 250mph. Stevens' gunners fired 600 rounds at the H8K, which, although damaged, continued to gradually pull away from the PB4Y. Stevens had to abandon the chase due to dwindling fuel.

The US Navy subsequently learned from sources in China that the "Emily" had crash-landed on a riverbank near the coast in an area under Nationalist Chinese control. When Chinese troops approached the stranded flying boat, several of its crew fought back, only to be killed. Rather than be taken prisoner, Vice-Admiral Yamagata committed suicide. By a strange coincidence, Yamagata was related to Osprey author Osamu Tagaya through his mother's family.

The string of PB4Y victories over IJNAF flying boats ended as they had begun, with a "Mavis" falling to the guns of a Liberator. During May 1945, VPB-116 was officially based at Tinian, but most of the squadron's aircraft were operating from Iwo Jima on patrols to the coast of Japan. On May 9, Lt Cdr Allen Waggoner, VPB-116's CO, left Iwo Jima early in the morning for a patrol along the coast of Honshu, east of Nagoya, searching for Japanese radar and radio stations.

Flying east across Suruga Bay, the crew sighted a Japanese aircraft heading south off their port bow, which they quickly identified as a "Mavis." Waggoner let it pass overhead and then turned to starboard to come in behind his victim. The PB4Y chased the H6K for 30 miles before getting into range. When the top turret gunner told Waggoner he was now close enough to open fire, Waggoner replied, "Okay, go ahead and get the son-of-a bitch."

The "Mavis" was still unaware that the PB4Y was approaching from below and behind, as it appears to have been an H6K transport variant with no tail turret. Waggoner moved his aircraft into a position just 100 yards behind and 75ft below the "Mavis," at which point the bow turret gunner, as instructed, directed his fire along the fuselage, while the top turret gunner targeted the engines. Moments later the No. 2 engine burst into flames. After two minutes of firing the "Mavis" nosed over and, with flames streaming from one wing, hit the water. The pilot appeared to have been attempting a landing, but after bouncing once upon making heavy contact with the sea, the aircraft exploded when it touched down for a second time.

The run of PB4Y claims against IJNAF flying boats ended as it began, with a Liberator shooting down a "Mavis." On May 9, 1945, VPB-116 CO Lt Cdr Allen Waggoner and his crew engaged an H6K transport off the coast of Japan. As can be clearly seen here, the patrol bomber's bow and top turret gunners set the flying boat's port wing ablaze in a series of bursts lasting two minutes in total. (80G-490083, RG80, NARA)

STATISTICS AND ANALYSIS

An analysis of the combats between the PB4Y and the H6K and H8K brings out the stark disparity in results. From the first engagement between these aircraft in 1943 to the last combat in 1945, the PB4Ys claimed 15 "Mavis" and "Emily" flying boats shot down, comprising five H6Ks and ten H8Ks. The PB4Y crews involved saw all but one of these Japanese aircraft crash.

During 1944, the US Navy claimed eight "Mavis" flying boats shot down, with the PB4Ys accounting for half of them, and 22 "Emilys," a third of which were claimed by the PB4Y squadrons. The PB4Y squadrons were credited with 24.6 percent of all Japanese flying boats claimed to have been shot down by the US Navy during the war. In turn, as far as can be determined, no PB4Ys were lost in combat with IJNAF flying boats.

The highest scoring squadron against the Japanese flying boats was VB/VPB-104, which claimed two H6Ks and one H8K shot down between August 1943 and March 1945. Four other squadrons – VB/VPB-106, VB/VPB-115, VPB-116, and VPB-117 – each claimed two flying boats destroyed. Lt Everett Mitchell and his crew from VB/VPB-106 was the only PB4Y crew to have claimed two flying boats (a "Mavis" and an "Emily"), downing both within a single week in a phenomenal run of luck given the infrequency of contacts between the patrol bombers and the IJNAF flying boats.

The question that arises from the evaluation of these numbers is why the results were so one-sided? The answer for the combats between the PB4Y and the "Mavis" is straightforward – the PB4Y was far superior in terms of firepower and protection,

After the end of the war, a Type 97 transport sits at the Dai Nippon Koku base at Yokohama opposite an H8K. The "Mavis" has been repainted in a standard surrender scheme, consisting of a white finish overall and green crosses. (GAF_image_804_1, MoF)

especially against the transport versions of the H6K, which had little chance of survival against a PB4Y. Its lack of protected fuel tanks and only limited armament made the "Mavis" vulnerable to any determined attack.

The H8K is the more intriguing case. The "Emily" had armor protection for the crew, the most effective self-sealing fuel tanks of any Japanese aircraft fielded in World War II, an additional CO_2 system to prevent fires, high speed and, most importantly, heavy armament of five 20mm cannon in the bow, waist, dorsal, and tail turrets. It was considered to be a difficult aircraft to shoot down. The weight of fire from a two-second burst from three Type 99 20mm cannon in an "Emily" was slightly greater than the weight of fire from a two-second burst from the four 0.50-cal Browning M2 machine guns in the bow and top turrets of a PB4Y. The heavier individual 20mm rounds were also more destructive than a 0.50-cal round. Yet despite these advantages, the H8K fared poorly against the PB4Y. A possible answer to the disparity may be found in differences in doctrine, tactics, and training, as well as a technical "fault" with the "Emily."

US Navy patrol bomber doctrine was resolutely offensive. While reconnaissance remained the primary mission of its flying boats and land-based patrol aircraft, offensive action against enemy shipping, aircraft and military installations was encouraged. The US Navy's patrol aircraft, both flying boats and land-based types, always had provision for carrying bombs and torpedoes, and they were expected to conduct offensive missions.

During the Pacific War, the US Navy's patrol bombing squadrons usually had a complement of 12 aircraft, with two to three more held in reserve. A single aircraft would average ten to 12 flights per month, and record an "action sortie" – one that resulted in an attack on an enemy target or enemy aircraft – in one out of eight flights. The PB4Ys carried bombs or depth charges on every patrol mission. Not surprisingly, more than 50 percent of the action sorties were against Japanese shipping, particularly smaller vessels of less than 500 tons.

The PB4Ys engaged 1,254 Japanese aircraft during their patrols, claiming 306 destroyed for the loss of 28 PB4Ys, with a further 99 damaged. This gave an overall victory-to-loss ratio of 10.9 Japanese aircraft for every PB4Y lost; the highest ratio among land-based US Navy and US Marine Corps aircraft. The PB4Ys claimed 125 Japanese bombers, transports, and flying boats destroyed, plus 181 fighters. Engagements with Japanese fighters were usually defensive battles, but the PB4Y was a hard nut for enemy fighters to crack. Between September 1944 and August 1945, the PB4Ys claimed 64 Japanese single-engined fighters shot down for the loss of 11 PB4Ys – a ratio close to six-to-one. Even with probable over-claiming in these combats, the PB4Ys gave as good as they received.

Against IJNAF floatplanes, flying boats, bombers, and transports, the PB4Y's dominance was absolute. During this same 1944–45 period, PB4Ys claimed 140 Japanese aircraft shot down without loss. The PB4Y pilots and crews were aggressive in their attacks.

The PB4Y squadrons developed effective tactics against Japanese flying boats, firstly in positioning and, secondly, in targeting. Pilots would attempt to maneuver their aircraft to come in behind a "Mavis" or "Emily" slightly off to one side and, to the extent possible, allow for multiple gun positions to fire on the enemy flying boat. In an analysis of PB4Y claims against Japanese aircraft for the period January to June 1944, multiple gunners participated in 73 percent of the successful combats. Not surprisingly, the bow and top turrets were involved in more than 50 percent of the engagements. Targeting was specific and precise. The PB4Y gunners learned to first shoot out the turrets of the "Mavis" and "Emily" flying boats they encountered. Having eliminated the threat of return fire, they could then target the vulnerable engines and fuel tanks. PB4Y gunners were excellent shots, as the Aircraft Action Reports describe. Once in range, destruction of an H6K or H8K rarely took more than a few minutes of intense fire. This speaks to the superiority of the US Navy's gunnery training.

In contrast, IJNAF patrol aircraft doctrine appears to have undergone a change in emphasis during the war. At the beginning of the conflict the IJNAF employed the H6K and later the H8K on bombing and torpedo missions, but the flying boat Kokutai eventually abandoned such operations to concentrate on reconnaissance and transport missions when the results of offensive sorties did not justify the losses incurred. This may have been due in part to the paucity of large flying boats available to the IJNAF as the war progressed.

Where the US Navy, during 1944–45, had an average of 371 patrol aircraft of all types available in the Pacific (PB4Y, PV, PBM, and PBY), the IJNAF may have had as few as 50 operational H8Ks shared between three flying boat Kokutai. With increasing operational losses and slowing production of replacement aircraft, the IJNAF had to disband the 802nd Kokutai in April 1944 and the 851st Kokutai seven months later, leaving only the 801st Kokutai as the primary Type 2 Flying Boat unit. Small numbers of H8Ks also served with the 901st, 951st, and Takuma Kokutai. With flying boats scarce, IJNAF doctrine shifted to conserving its available aircraft, rather than risking them in offensive operations.

This sense of risk-aversion may have also been an influence in Japanese flying boat tactics when under attack. The Aircraft Action Reports from the PB4Y crews repeatedly state that there was minimal evasive action taken on the part of the flying boats once they were engaged. The main tactic appears to have been seeking to escape from the attacking PB4Y, descending toward the ocean (where most encounters took place) to protect the vulnerable underside of the flying boat and to increase speed to outrun the attacking American aircraft. Even so, in most engagements the PB4Y was able to chase down even the faster "Emily" – H8K pilots did not push their aircraft to their limit soon enough. Only on a few occasions did an "Emily" pilot aggressively maneuver his flying boat in an attempt to foil an attack.

The most puzzling aspect of these combats is the consistently and exceptionally poor gunnery from the IJNAF crews. It is astonishing how the gunners manning weapons in the Japanese flying boats, particularly the "Emily," not only failed to damage an attacking PB4Y but never actually managed to hit the patrol bomber at all. The most glaring example – no doubt a great relief to the PB4Y crew involved – came on October 31, 1944 when an "Emily's" 20mm turrets fired off an estimated 200+ rounds and achieved just a single hit on the chasing Liberator.

Despite the H8K's heavy-hitting armament, the crews did not seem able to take advantage of the power of their weapons. This raises questions about the nature and quality of Japanese gunnery training, or at least the gunnery training the IJNAF provided to its flying boat crews. Similarly, there is a question as to what form of training Japanese flying boat pilots received for countering air attacks.

What also comes out of the Aircraft Action Reports are the repeated examples of the PB4Y's 0.50-cal guns rapidly setting the H8K's engines on fire. From the reports it seems apparent that the protection for the "Emily's" fuel tanks was, in the main, successful, as the accounts frequently express the frustration of the PB4Y crews in not seeing the flying boat burst into flame after hits in the fuel tanks as with other Japanese aircraft. It may well be that while the IJNAF took steps to protect the H8K's fuel system, it seems to have ignored the engines, thus inadvertently creating an area of vulnerability.

PB4Y claims against the "Mavis" and "Emily" in 1943–45			
Squadron	H6K "Mavis"	H8K "Emily"	Total Claims
VB/VPB-104	2	1	3
VB/VPB-106	1	1	2
VB/VPB-115		2	2
VPB-116	1	1	2
VPB-117		2	2
VB/VPB-101		1	1
VB/VPB-108		1	1
VB/VPB-109	1		1
VPB-118		1	1

AFTERMATH

The US Navy chose to bring an H8K back to the USA for extensive testing. After selecting the best example, the flying boat was shipped to NAS Whidbey Island, Washington, on board the seaplane tender USS *Cumberland Sound* (AV-17) in November 1945. The aircraft is seen here at the Naval Air Station's Oak Harbor facility, with three PBM5 Mariners behind it on their beaching gear. US Navy personnel thoroughly examined the "Emily" at Oak Harbor and determined it could not be flown cross country to the test center at NAS Patuxent River. (80G-278283, RG80, NARA)

By the end of 1944, the IJNAF's H8Ks were resorting to night time reconnaissance (using their ASV radar to locate the US Navy's carrier fleets) so as to avoid daytime interceptions from American patrol aircraft and carrier fighters. The growing complement of F6F nightfighters embarked in US Navy carriers and flying from land bases made even night flights hazardous for the "Emily" crews tasked with seeking out the Fast Carrier Task Force sailing off Japan and Okinawa.

As detailed earlier, on March 11, 1945, two H8Ks escorted 25 P1Y1 "Frances" bombers in an ultimately unsuccessful attack on the US Navy fleet anchorage at Ulithi, and this proved to be the "Emily's" last major operation. In the fighting over the Japanese home islands and around Okinawa from March to May 1945, US Navy carrier aircraft claimed five H8Ks shot down, four of them at night, and four more destroyed in strafing attacks. The IJNAF grouped its few remaining "Emilys" in the Takuma Kokutai based on the Inland Sea. All told, in the final six months of the war, the IJNAF lost 25 of the 28 H8Ks it had on strength in Japan. Remarkably, one survived the war and is now on display in a museum in Japan.

Following the Japanese surrender, the US Navy was keen to acquire an H8K for testing, and it found three serviceable examples at Takuma naval base. The aircraft that was subsequently selected had served with the 802nd Kokutai in the Central Pacific. With the help of IJNAF groundcrew and an "Emily" pilot, the US Navy had the flying boat flown to Yokohama, south of Tokyo. From here, the H8K was transported by ship across the Pacific to NAS Whidbey Island, north of Seattle,

The US Navy shipped the "Emily" to Norfolk and made the last flight of a Type 2 Flying Boat up to NAS Patuxent River, where the flying boat underwent hydrodynamic testing. Fortunately, the US Navy preserved the aircraft and ultimately returned it to Japan. (80G-265581, RG80, NARA)

Washington, where an examination revealed it was not in an airworthy condition to fly across the USA. Instead, the flying boat was shipped through the Panama Canal to NAS Norfolk, Virginia, arriving in May 1946.

Two Naval Aviators duly made the final flight of an H8K, flying from Norfolk to NAS Patuxent River (the US Navy's flight test center) in Maryland, losing two engines on the way and a third on landing. Once repaired, the aircraft commenced hydrodynamic tests in August 1946, which were completed by January 1947. The US Navy then returned the aircraft to NAS Norfolk, where it went into storage.

In 1959, while visiting research facilities in the USA, Dr. Shizuo Kikuhara, who had designed the H8K, visited the "Emily," which was wrapped in a rubber coating to protect the flying boat from the elements. His visit led to an effort to return it to Japan. This finally happened in 1979, when the "Emily" was presented to the Tokyo Museum of Maritime Science. After two years of restoration, it went on public view, remaining at the Museum until 2004, when the Japan Defense Agency took ownership of the flying boat and moved it to the Japan Maritime Self-Defense Force (JMSDF) base at Kanoya, near Kagoshima, on the island of Kyushu. The aircraft is presently on display there as part of the JMSDF Museum.

The H8K's legacy also lived on in the Shin Meiwa PS-1/US-1 flying boats built for the JMSDF. At the end of the war, the Allied occupation authorities disbanded the large Japanese industrial groups and prohibited aircraft production. The Kawanishi Company was dissolved, only to reform in 1949 as the Shin Meiwa Industry Company, Ltd. to build heavy machinery. It also undertook work for the US Air Force during the Korean War.

Although many of the company's aircraft engineers had found work elsewhere following the dissolution of Kawanishi, Dr. Shizuo Kikuhara stayed on, and during the 1950s he headed up a committee researching flying boat designs. Although the large flying boat was by then rapidly losing favor with many navies, Dr. Kikuhara and his team developed the PS-1 for the JMSDF. The aircraft boasted short take-off and landing features and good seaworthiness, the latter being achieved in part through spray suppression strakes that

The legacy of the Type 2 Flying Boat lived on in the Shin Meiwa PS-1/US-1 flying boat designed for the JMSDF by Dr. Shizuo Kikuhara, who created the H8K. The US-1A air-sea rescue variant, an example of which is seen here, served with the JMSDF's Air Rescue Squadron 71 at Atsugi Air Base until 2017, when the aircraft was replaced by the improved US-2. (Wikipedia/CC BY 4.0)

were derived from those fitted to the H8K. The JMSDF acquired 23 PS-1s, which served until 1989.

Dr. Kikuhara also designed an amphibious version of the PS-1 for air-sea search and rescue, designated the US-1 and modified US-1A. Shin Meiwa (renamed ShinMaywa in 1992) built 14 of these aircraft. In 2004 the company developed an improved amphibious search and rescue aircraft, designated the US-2, which remains in service with the JMSDF.

During the final few months of the war, the US Navy steadily added PB4Y-2 Privateer squadrons to its Fleet Air Wings in the Pacific. In August 1945 there were eight Privateer squadrons based on Okinawa, in the Mariana Islands, and in the Philippines, with five more units still flying the PB4Y-1 or converting to the PB4Y-2. After the war Privateers replaced Liberators in the US Navy's land-based patrol squadrons. The Privateers flew signals intelligence missions off the coasts of the Soviet Union and the People's Republic of China, and during the Korean War dropped flares supporting night attacks on enemy convoys. The US Navy's weather squadrons used Privateers to chase hurricanes in the Caribbean and typhoons in the Pacific. The PB4Y-2 served with the regular US Navy until 1954, and then with US Naval Reserve squadrons for a few more years. The US Coast Guard acquired a small number of Privateers modified for search and rescue, operating these aircraft until 1958.

Several foreign air arms also acquired the PB4Y-2s, notably the French *Aéronavale*, which used the aircraft for patrol and search and rescue missions during the colonial wars in Indochina and Algeria. Called on to support beleaguered French forces at Dien Bien Phu, the *Aéronavale* equipped some of its PB4Y-2s with Norden bombsights, losing two aircraft on these missions. The PB4Y-2 also saw combat with the air force of the Republic of China, the Nationalist Chinese receiving 38 aircraft for patrols, harassing raids on the People's Republic and clandestine missions to drop agents over the mainland and in northern Burma. The People's Liberation Army Air Force shot down a PB4Y-2 that was bombing the city of Xiamen on September 12, 1954, while on February 14, 1961, the Nationalists lost a second PB4Y-2 over Burma, shot down by a Burmese Air Force Sea Fury.

After the end of their military service, many former PB4Y-2s went to commercial operators. Re-engined with Wright R-2600 Cyclone 14s, a number served as fire bombers dropping flame retardant on forest fires until retired in 2002. While a few Privateers are on view in several American aviation museums, no PB4Y-1s have survived.

The PB4Y-2 Privateer had a long career with the US Navy, the US Coast Guard, and with foreign air forces post-war. In 1951, the US Navy re-designated its remaining PB4Y-2s as P4Y-2s. This photograph shows a line of P4Y-2s of VP-9 at NAS Barbers Point, Hawaii. VP-9's Privateers participated in the Korean War, dropping flares for US Marine Corps nightfighters. (80G-443411, RG80, NARA)

FURTHER READING

BOOKS

Burindo, *Famous Aircraft of the World No. 49 – Type 2 Flying Boat* (Bunrindo, 1994)

Carey, Alan C., *Above an Angry Sea – United States Navy B-24 Liberator and PB4Y-2 Privateer Operations in the Pacific October 1944–August 1945* (Schiffer Publishing, 2001)

Carey, Alan C., *Consolidated-Vultee PB4Y-2 Privateer – The Operational History of the US Navy's World War II Patrol/Bomber Aircraft* (Schiffer Publishing, 2005)

Carey, Alan C., *The Reluctant Raiders – The Story of United States Navy Bombing Squadron VB/VPB-109 in World War II* (Schiffer Publishing, 1999)

Carey, Alan C., *We Flew Alone – United States Navy B-24 Squadrons in the Pacific February 1943-September 1944* (Schiffer Publishing, 2000)

Ginter, Steve, *Naval Fighters No. 93 – Convair PB4Y-2/P4Y-2 Privateer* (Steve Ginter, 2012)

Ginter, Steve, *Naval Fighters Number 105 – Consolidated PB4Y-1/1P Liberator* (Steve Ginter, 2017)

Hitsuji, Tsuneo, *Saigo no Hikotai – Kaigun Hikotai Eiko no Kiroku* (The Last Flying Boat – A Record of Glory of the Navy's Flying Boats) (1983)

Kittrell, Ed, *Solo Into the Rising Sun – The Dangerous Missions of a US Navy Bomber Squadron in World War II* (Stackpole Books, 2020)

Nohara, Shigeru and Kazuo Iinuma, *Aero Detail 31 – Kawanishi H8K "Emily" Type 2 Flying Boat*, (Dainippon Kaiga Co., Ltd., 2003)

Peattie, Mark R., *Sunburst – The Rise of Japanese Naval Air Power, 1909–1941* (Naval Institute Press, 2001)

Pettit, James T., *VPB-118 – The History of Navy Bombing Squadron 118 "The Old Crows"* (James T. Pettit, 1991)

Richards, M. C., *Aircraft Profile 233 – Kawanishi 4-Motor Flying-Boats (H6K 'Mavis' and H8K 'Emily'* (Profile Publications, Ltd, 1972)

Stevens, Paul F., *Low Level Liberators – The Story of Patrol Bombing Squadron 104 in the South Pacific during World War II*, (P. F. Stevens, 1997)

Thompson, Harry J., *The Buccaneers of Harry Sears – The History of Navy Bombing Squadron 104 World War II, April 1943 to April 1944, Solomons*, (H. J. Thompson, 1997)

White, Ian, *Warpaint Series No. 96 – Consolidated B-24 Liberator*, (Guideline Publications, 2014)

PERIODICALS

"Kawanishi's Parasol Patroller," *Air International Vol. 29, No. 6*, pp.293–298, 304–305 (December 1985)

"Kawanishi Type 2 Flying Boat (H8K)," *The Maru Mechanic Extra Edition* (1984)

Green, William and Gordon Swanborough, "The Unrivalled Emily," *Air International* Vol. 24, No. 4, pp.179–187 (April 1983)

Raithel, Capt Albert L., "Patrol Aviation in the Pacific in WWII, Part 1," *Naval Aviation News Vol. 74, No. 5*, pp.32–37 (July–August 1992)

Raithel, Capt Albert L., "Patrol Aviation in the Pacific in WWII, Part 2," *Naval Aviation News Vol. 74, No. 6*, pp.30–35 (September–October 1992)

Stevens, Paul F., "The Catch of the Day," *Naval History Magazine, Vol. 3, No. 2* (April 1989)

INDEX